SO-BFB-868

6/00

COLLECTOR'S GUIDE TO

HULL POTTERY

THE DINNERWARE LINES

IDENTIFICATION & VALUES

Barbara Loveless Gick-Burke

COLLECTOR BOOKS

A Division of Schroeder Publishing Co., Inc.

The current values in this book should be used only as a guide. They are not intended to set prices, which vary from one section of the country to another. Auction prices as well as dealer prices vary greatly and are affected by condition as well as demand. Neither the Author nor the Publisher assumes responsibility for any losses that might be incurred as a result of consulting this guide.

Photography by Beverly Brosius

On The Cover:
Top Left: Gingerbread Man Cookie Jar (Gray) $175.00-220.00
Top Right: Imperial Swan Centerpiece (Tangerine) $25.00-40.00
Bottom Left: Imperial Rose Pitcher (Dark Green) $15.00-22.00
Bottom Middle: Imperial Vase (Tangerine) $14.00-19.00
Bottom Right: Ring Coffee Pot (Mirror Brown) $40.00-50.00

Searching For A Publisher?

We are always looking for knowledgeable people considered to be experts within their fields. If you feel that there is a real need for a book on your collectible subject and have a large comprehensive collection, contact us.

COLLECTOR BOOKS
P.O. Box 3009
Paducah, Kentucky 42002-3009

Additional copies of this book may be ordered from:

COLLECTOR BOOKS
P.O. Box 3009
Paducah, Kentucky 42002-3009

@$16.95. Add $2.00 for postage and handling.

Copyright: Barbara Loveless Gick-Burke, 1993

This book or any part thereof or may not be reproduced without the written consent of the Author and Publisher.

1 2 3 4 5 6 7 8 9 0

Printed by IMAGE GRAPHICS, INC., Paducah, Kentucky

TABLE OF CONTENTS

ACKNOWLEDGMENTS

My heartfelt "Thanks" to the special people who helped me with the completion of this manuscript;

First to my mother, Charlotte Loveless of Sullivan, Indiana, whose encouragement and support were the mainstay of my motivation to continue when the task seemed too daunting; not to mention whose involvement in antiques as a long-time dealer influenced my interest in collecting in the first place.

Second to my husband, Bill, who jokingly notes the fact that his "bachelor" home was immediately and totally filled overnight with hundreds of pieces of pottery, the trappings of a 12-year-old child, research materials, a computer and an endless stream of strangers; and who not only accepted the changes gracefully but with a great sense of humor for which I love him dearly.

Third to my son, Jereme, who has often stated through this long and exhausting project, that his mother "was attached to that computer"; but who, despite his personal sacrifices of hot meals and special attention, has been heard to brag to his friends about his mother's collection and her book.

Last but not Least, to those special people like my good friend, Martha Urey of Orlando, who has shared this project with me from the beginning, and who, along with Robby Keefer, worked through the long and tiring photographic sessions to carry pottery, clean spots and repack between shots; to Mike Hood of St. Louis, Missouri for helping me find special pieces for the book and for becoming a friend in the process; to Beverly Brosius of Winter Park, Florida who did such a splendid job on the photography; to Harvey Duke of Brooklyn, New York. and Joan Gray Hull of Huron, South Dakota. for taking time away from their current projects to offer their advise and support; and to Larry Taylor of Crooksville, Ohio to whom I owe a great debt for all the helpful information, insight and materials provided to assist me with this manuscript....no single word of thanks can ever repay my indebtedness for all his help!

And I cannot forget to mention the wonderful new friends I found who also love and collect this great pottery, like Debby Spriggs, Stella Frash, Cindy Mountz, and Carolyn Trotter whose excitement and encouragement keep me going to this day.

Finally to Lori Friend who has worked so hard to support me in this project...and whose love of this pottery is equal to mine.... and who has become my very best friend!

THANKS TO ALL OF YOU!

FROM THE AUTHOR

It all began innocently enough on a rainy day 12 years ago with a duck. Not, mind you, one of the feathered types; but rather the Brown-Drip casserole variety.......the Hull House 'n Garden Duck.

I first laid eyes on him on a gray drizzly day at an estate auction in Indiana. He looked so lonely and out of place on the back of the farm trailer where he waited in the rain with other more colorful items for a new owner. He grabbed my heart...and little did I know then....my life.

My Hull House 'n Garden Duck went home with me for the bargain price of $5.00. My poor orphan duck was not alone for long; however, for soon thereafter I stumbled into an old country store that carried the Hull dinnerware from years long past. I was delighted to discover what has now become my obsession....that my lovely duck was a member of the huge family of Hull House 'n Garden dinnerware!

As my collection grew...a chicken here, an oil and vinegar set there... I learned more about its origins and the factory in Crooksville, Ohio that produced this wonderful pottery. My interest led me to contact the Hull factory and to begin negotiations to outlet the dinnerware in Florida. Unfortunately, prior to getting my first order together, the factory closed. As an already avid Hull collector, I was understandably sad, but, knowing the source was severed, I redoubled my efforts and collected with even more enthusiasm. And I am, still to this day, enthralled with each and every new and prized acquisition.

My collection today consists of over 1000 pieces. My original duck, two chickens, a rooster, a gingerbread cookie jar and numerous pitchers, platters and centerpieces grace my cabinet ledges. My counter tops are strewn with canisters, piggy banks, vases, cookie jars and salt & pepper sets. I eat on it, cook with it in the microwave and the oven, store food in it in the refrigerator and wash it in the dishwasher...so my collection is not only fun but practical!

The fact that the House 'n Garden and related lines were produced for over 25 years in huge quantities makes collecting more affordable....a large supply exists to keep prices down. The dinnerware was distributed in the U.S., Canada and as far away as Australia. For a time, J.C. Penny outlet the pottery through its chain stores and catalog sales. The dinnerware was also sold in other discount stores throughout the country. Over the years, Hull dinnerware has migrated to every corner of the nation; thus it can be found in antique stores, yard sales and thrift stores from Maine to California. And because there were so many varied and interesting molds used in the production of this dinnerware; i.e., the unusual animal shaped serving dishes and the numerous pitchers and centerpieces of all sizes and shapes; collecting is always exciting! After 12 years, I am still surprised and delighted to find "new" items for my collection!

Limited production or test runs, employee specials and limited circulation of some items add to the mystique surrounding the history and availability of these dinnerware lines.

I have attempted to cover as many of the mold variations as possible in this publication, as well as, to address the scope of colors used in the production of the various dinnerware lines represented in this book. While there have been several publications previously on the collector book market, no one publication has addressed this segment of Hull pottery production in depth. As the dinnerware lines were in production longer and in greater quantities than any other of the Hull pottery lines and were the only production lines in the last few years the Hull Pottery Company operated; I feel that it is time to recognize this "stepchild" of Hull ...previously neglected in favor of the more popular art pottery.

In regard to pricing, I have endeavored to reflect the collector value for the dinnerware as exists in the marketplace today. I do not, by this publication, attempt to establish market value; but only to create a guideline for collectors and dealers who are unfamiliar with this dinnerware. I have used pricing information from dealers and collectors alike from all areas of the country to arrive at the price guidelines in this publication. Because some areas have more plentiful supplies than others, the price for a single item may vary by as much as 50%, thus I have indicated the value representing these variations. But keep in mind, the value of an item is not established by the book or the dealer, but by the buyer....as my mother, who has been a successful antique dealer in Indiana for many years, has always told me...."The value is what it is worth to you to buy it....how much you feel comfortable spending to own it." So if the value exceeds your price comfort zone, and detracts from your joy of ownership, then the price is probably too high! You, as the collector, must weigh your desire to acquire a piece with your comfort with the cost.

However, if you have recently joined the ranks of the Hull House 'n Garden dinnerware collectors, take heart in the fact that it is a relatively new "collectible" and the availability is still good. And, while the pricing varies from one area of the country to another, it still falls well below price levels of most other collectible dinnerware lines. Thus, a beginning collector can hope to add treasured pieces to his collection without overburdening his pocket book!

So, happy hunting...... but before I close I would like to leave you with this thought......The joy of collecting is inspired by the artistry of the collection....and the creators of Hull pottery were truly gifted artists to have created such beautiful and timeless earthenware.

Barbara Burke
Orlando, Florida

A BRIEF HISTORY OF HULL POTTERY

The A.E. Hull Pottery Company was formed in July of 1905 in Crooksville, Ohio. Due to the natural clay deposits in the region as a ready source of raw materials, Ohio has boasted many pottery companies over the last century. Some of the potteries that operated in this region are well known among collectors. The McCoy Pottery Company, to name one, operated in Roseville, Ohio until a fire destroyed the factory in 1991.

Addis Emmet Hull, one of the principal founders, began his career as a salesman for his brother, J.J. Hull, who managed the Star Stonery Company, an Ohio stoneware manufacturer. Striking out to form his own enterprise, he formed The Globe Pottery Company in 1901 and operated this plant until 1904 when he sold his interests and became involved in the organization of the A.E. Hull Pottery Company.

In 1907 the A.E. Hull Pottery Company acquired the Acme Pottery Company expanding its operations to include both plants and over 300 employees. It was the beginning of the pottery's long and successful manufacturing history.

From 1907 until June of 1950, the pottery manufactured various kitchen and hotel ware and novelty ware and the art pottery lines which are so collectible today. Much has been written regarding this period of Hull production, and many fine publications are available that reference the pottery manufactured during this time.

Disaster struck on June 16, 1950 when a flood caused the kilns of the pottery company to explode. The subsequent fire destroyed the kilns, the building and all business records, effectively ending the 50-year-old pottery manufacturing business. However, due to the past success of the factory and the determination of its owners and stockholders, the factory was rebuilt and new molds and glazes were formulated. Production resumed in the new building early 1952, but the name of the pottery was then changed from the A.E. Hull Pottery Company to the Hull Pottery Company. James Brannon Hull was elected president, with Robert W. Hull appointed as vice president.

Unable to reconstruct the formulas for the glazes used in the manufacturing process prior to the destruction of the factory, the pottery was forced to change its manufacturing strategies. During the 50's, a large volume of novelty items and kitchenware was produced in addition to the art pottery lines. During this period the factory experimented with issues of the Crescent Kitchenware, Heritageware and Marcrest kitchen lines. These lines were limited, however, and it wasn't until the early 1960's that the Hull Pottery Company began production of its first complete dinnerware lines...the House 'n Garden serving ware!

Because many in-depth publications already exist detailing the history of the factory's production of the pottery lines prior to 1960, including their subsequent art pottery and novelty lines; the focus of this publication is directed to the dinnerware lines manufactured after 1960 of which there has been little recognition.

HULL'S HOUSE 'N GARDEN
DINNERWARE HISTORY

The first production of the heavy, oven-proof dinnerware was manufactured in the original Mirror Brown and trimmed with the white/ivory foam drip; however, within the next year, Hull introduced its Rainbow serving ware, adding Tangerine, Green Agate and Butterscotch to their list of available glazes. The Rainbow colors were produced for the basic starter set along with additional companion serving pieces through 1967.

One short-lived line named Provincial was manufactured in these early days, however, due to the difficulty in applying the half-tone glazes, the line was discontinued shortly after its introduction. There are only a few survivors of this dinnerware line, and pieces are highly prized. Also during these years, the Tangerine and Green Agate were offered as full dinnerware lines with individual brochures printed for each color. While the Tangerine serving ware remained part of the House 'n Garden line, the Green Agate was named Country Squire and the Provincial molds were incorporated for the mixing bowls. However, neither the Tangerine or the Country Squire were offered in the full array of molds available in the Mirror Brown House 'n Garden line.

In March of 1965, a whole new line of molds were introduced as Crestone and marketed as an oven-proof creation for casual living. This new color, a mix between bird's egg blue and turquoise, represented what many feel was Hull's attempt to create a dinnerware line that would appeal to those interested in the Art Deco style. With the exception of the butter dish and coffee mug, these new molds had sharper and more modern lines. The 2-cup coffee Carafe was introduced at this time along with its companion 7 oz. stacking coffee cup. However, the line did not experience much success and production was discontinued in 1967.

Shortly after the Crestone introduction, Hull also introduced the House 'n Garden molds in Avocado with the standard ivory trim. Both the original House 'n Garden molds and the Crestone molds were used in the production of this line. It was offered as a starter set #604 containing the original House 'n Garden starter set molds, and as #670 containing the Crestone molds. The Crestone molds were not altered to produce the brown glaze, and in fact, many of these House 'n Garden pieces are found with the Crestone imprint. Avocado was in production from 1968 through 1971, making it second in production quantities to House 'n Garden Mirror Brown.

The Rainbow, Crestone and Avocado lines were discontinued in 1967 when all focus was directed toward the House 'n Garden Mirror Brown.

From 1967 through to the early 80's, Hull continued to produce the Mirror Brown dinnerware, adding new molds and discontinuing others, as well as, incorporating the Crestone molds into this production. During this period, however, many experimental colors were produced both officially and unofficially. Employees often created special items or glazes for existing molds for their personal use, and many of these items are still found today....thus making it impossible to state that any particular mold cannot be found in any one of the many glazes manufactured over the 20 plus years of production. Also, some of the test items include colors that never made it into production, such as the bright yellow creamer displayed with the experimental and test pieces that are included in this publication.

When new management was installed in 1981, the direction of the pottery's production again changed. New molds and glazes were added in an attempt to create more marketable products to boost lagging sales. (More about the change in management and the economic plight of the pottery in the following article about Larry Taylor, president of Hull Pottery.) Mirror Almond was produced for a short time during this period.

It was during these final years that Hull introduced the Ridge lines. In an effort to modernize its dinnerware production, Hull created these new molds and offered them in Flint Ridge (Gray), Tawny Ridge (Sand) and Walnut Ridge (Brown). In addition to the new molds and colors, Hull retained many of its more popular House 'n Garden molds such as the Duck and Chicken Casseroles, the 64 oz. Coffee Pot, 72 oz. Ice Jug and 80 oz. Water Jug, to name a few, and also produced these old favorites in the gray and sand colors.

In an effort to compete with Pfaltzgraff (the pottery company that had won the J.C. Penney's business from Hull), Hull also produced new molds for their Heartland and Country Belle lines. The resemblance to Pfaltzgraff is not surprising considering it was designed by free-lance designer Maury Mountain, that also designed for Pfaltzgraff! These new lines offered a new dimension to the pottery production by incorporating painted decorations into their finished products. Again, Hull included some of the more popular House 'n Garden molds into this production...and the Duck and Chicken Casseroles were included in these lines. These same molds were also produced in the mirror brown glaze, however, this line was not officially named. These lines were not manufactured for long however, due to the closing of the plant, and these pieces are very difficult to find.

Also, during these final years, the Hull Pottery production included their popular Gingerbread line which consisted of the Gingerbread Man Cookie Jar, Gingerbread Man Server, Gingerbread Boy Coaster/Spoon Rest (all manufactured in the brown, gray and sand), as well as, the Gingerbread Child's Cup and Bowl which were manufactured only in the brown.

(Note: subsequent to the closing of the factory, many of the Gingerbread Man Cookie Jars were manufactured under a subcontract with Western Stoneware, an Illinois pottery, due to the worker's strike. In fact, Western Stoneware continues to produce Limited Edition items today.)

An addition to the Gingerbread line, the much sought after Gingerbread Train Canister Set was manufactured in a very limited quantity prior to the closing of the factory. While factory records indicate only approximately 16 complete Train Sets were manufactured, collectors claim approximately 30 complete sets exist in the original brown glaze. None of these sets were completed for sale, however, but were test pieces, and thus had not yet been marked with the Hull imprint.

One other piece that had been designed to complete the Gingerbread line was the Train Depot. This piece was only manufactured as a test item prior to the closing of the factory. And until December of 1991, this single test piece was in possession of Larry Taylor. Since that time, the Train Depot has been manufactured as a Limited Edition item by Mr. Taylor.

The factory was closed in 1985 after all efforts to revitalize failed.

THE FINAL YEARS
A MEETING WITH LARRY TAYLOR

I met with Larry Taylor, president of Hull Pottery, in October of 1991. Mr. Taylor and his family have lived in Crooksville, Ohio for over 25 years. In fact, his current residence is within a few blocks of the Hull plant. He graciously agreed to meet with me to talk about his tenure as president and to offer some insight into the plant operations as they existed during his management of the company, and the events leading up to the plant closure.

When Larry Taylor came on board as president of Hull Pottery Company on May 26, 1981, to take over the position previously held by Henry Sullens, the company had not had any new accounts in over seven years. In fact, according to Mr. Taylor, the company actually lost $10,000 the first month he was there! It was an unsettling beginning for the new management team made up of Larry Taylor and Jack Frame. Mr. Frame was the vice-president and plant superintendent, having joined Hull Pottery with Mr. Taylor.

In Mr. Taylor's opinion, several factors had come into play to bring about the decline of the company. The fact that there were no heirs to the Hull family line attributed to the lack of enthusiasm by the previous management (made up primarily of A.E. Hull's descendants) to promote future growth for the company. No effort had been made in the preceding years to establish new national accounts to replace the J.C. Penney account that was lost in 1978 after a three month strike. Previous to the strike of 1978, J.C. Penney had been Hull's largest dinnerware account, and the primary outlet for the factory's pottery production. J.C. Penney had never been satisfied with the ability of Hull Pottery to fill its discount store and catalog orders, and the strike was the final blow to their business relationship. After severing its ties to Hull, J.C. Penney went to the Pfaltzgraff company for its pottery dinnerware lines.

Another factor that was a direct result of the lack of interest in future growth was previous management's failure to upgrade equipment. The factory's kiln desperately needed to be replaced when production fell. The kiln was set up to operate 24 hours a day for a rotating shift. There was no way to shut it off when the additional shifts were not running. The cost for fuel to keep the kiln at the 1900 to 2000 degrees needed to fire the pottery was $10,000 a month. It was apparent to the new management team that a major overhaul needed to be made if the pottery was going to survive.

While Larry Taylor and Jack Frame were busy reviewing the company's position and planning its future, problems with the Environmental Protection Agency arose. Shortly after they had assumed their new responsibilities, a letter was received from the E.P.A. admonishing the company for its failure to comply with a previous edict to clean up the slush pond and surrounding grounds of unacceptable lead contamination. (Up to that time, the finishing glazes used in the firing of the pottery contained lead.) No record could be found of any previous correspondence from the E.P.A.; but the E.P.A. could not be persuaded that the company's failure to comply with their clean-up order was not intentional. As a result, a $100,000 fine was imposed on Hull Pottery. The company spent a great deal of its cash reserves to clean up the contaminated soil and change the glaze to eliminate the lead. Eight truck loads of contaminated soil were removed at a dumping cost of $8,000 per load. Lawyers were engaged and the negotiations continued for the next nine years until the fine was eventually reduced to a $22,000 cash settlement. In fact, the E.P.A.'s file on Hull Pottery was not actually closed until February of 1991! But the company had already invested over a quarter of a million dollars in legal fees and clean-up costs in the interim.

Meanwhile, the company was making an effort to establish new lines to attract new national accounts. It was during these last years that the Ridge lines were produced, followed by the Heartland and Country Belle lines, all of which were created with new molds. Over $250,000 was spent in the development and production of these molds for the new lines. What cash reserves were left were severely depleted by the development of these new lines in a last ditch effort to salvage the company.

The union strike in 1985 was the final factor in the decline and closure of the plant. Negotiations had been on-going with the factory's union representatives up to the final days before the strike. The representatives were brought in to review the company's books by Mr. Taylor in an effort to convince the workers that reductions were needed in the company's benefit programs in order to reduce overhead and continue operations. (By that time there were only 24 full-time workers at the facility.) But the union representatives were not convinced and a meeting was called for the strike vote. Many of the workers who were laid off, in addition to the working employees, felt that strike benefits paid by the union were better than no benefits at all, and so the vote was taken and a strike was ordered.

To add to the problems of the already overburdened company, the E.P.A. had come back for further testing and found that the soil surrounding the slush pond was still contaminated beyond acceptable E.P.A. levels.

Compounding the continuing E.P.A. problem was the fact that the pottery's cash reserves were exhausted. The workers were on strike and no new accounts had been established upon which to project future profits. No resources or projected revenues remained to justify continuing operations.

It was with a heavy heart that Mr. Taylor finally ordered the closing of the factory on August 5, 1985.

The equipment was sold to a Mr. Bill Skinner of Clarendon Ceramics. The building was closed. An auction was held to dispose of the stores of existing pottery. The end of an era had come for the Hull Pottery Company.

The real heros of Hull Pottery, according to Mr. Taylor, were the employees. Hull was a family operation. The workers cared about one another and the company they worked for. For the people of Crooksville and the employees of Hull Pottery, the closing of the plant was a devastating blow. Their loss was more than economic, it was personal and felt deeply by the community. The town has never fully recovered.

The people of Crooksville still reminisce fondly over stories of the glory days of the plant and their voices are edged with that particular sadness you hear when one talks of a lost loved one.

HOUSE 'N GARDENS BROWN DRIP
The Largest & Oldest Dinnerware Line

When The Hull Pottery Company began production of the House 'n Garden line in the early 60's, little did anyone at the factory suspect that this line would survive for over two decades! In fact, until the new molds of the latter years were introduced, the original starter set in this issue was still offered in the early 80's. The coffee pot, tea pot and beverage jugs were produced in such large quantities to be sold for restaurant ware that they are by far the easiest items to acquire. The #5850 Chicken and #5280 Duck casseroles were produced in the original mirror brown w/ivory foam trim through the 80's and also carried over into Heartland and Country Belle lines. The Sitting and Corky Pig Banks also were manufactured through the 80's and were also offered with the Ridge lines in gray and sand.

This original line is by far the most easily acquired due to the years it was in production and large volumes manufactured. This line also was the largest in the number of molds produced and contains some of the most interesting dinnerware accessories, such as the unusual animal shaped casseroles, the fancy chip 'n dip sets and leaf serving dishes. While many collectors shy away from the brown drip because of its color, most dinnerware collectors begin their collections with this line because of the quantity and variety of molds available.

I have displayed the dinner plates with both a front and back view on the next page in order that the beginning collector will be familiar with the differences in the molds used.

Row 1: #599 Luncheon Plate, 9⅜"

This mold was introduced into the House 'n Garden line after the production of the Crestone line, and some plates can be found with the "Crestone" imprint as the plate pictured on the far right, while later productions were remarked "Oven Proof" as the one displayed on the far left.

Row 2: #500 Dinner Plate, 10¼", Front and Back

From the original starter set, this mold is easily recognized by the rings located on the underside as shown by the plate on the right.

Row 3: #501 Salad Plate, 6½"
Front and Back

#531 Luncheon Plate, 8½"
Front and Back

These molds are miniatures of the #500 dinner plate mold.

Row 1:

   #509   Water Jug, 5 Pt.

   #522   Coffee Pot w/cover, 8 Cup

   #514   Ice Jug, 2 Qt.

Row 2:

   #525   Water Jug, 2 Pint

   #549   Tea Pot, 5 Cup

   #572   Jumbo Stein, 32 Oz. (Difficult to Find)

   #526   Beer Stein, 16 Oz.

   #571   Continental Mug, 10 Oz. (Difficult to Find)

Rare Condiment Set
#871 H*

Row 3:

   #516   Pepper Shaker w/cork, 3¾" High

   #515   Salt Shaker w/cork, 3¾" High

   #596   Table Size Salt & Pepper Shakers, (Unmarked)

   #587   Mushroom Salt Shaker, 3¾" High

   #588   Mushroom Pepper Shaker, 3¾" High

   #519   Sugar Bowl, 12 Oz.

   #518   Creamer or Jug, 8 Oz.

Row 4:

   #502   Mug, 9 Oz.

   #598   Saucer 5⅞"

   #597   Coffee Cup, 7 Oz.

   #505   Carafe w/cover, 2 Cup; (Fits #597 Cup)

   #529   Coffee Cup, 6 Oz. (From Rainbow Line)

   #530   Saucer, 5½" (From Rainbow Line)

Rare Serving Set
#872 H*

*Possibly for Austrailian "Home Party" Sales.

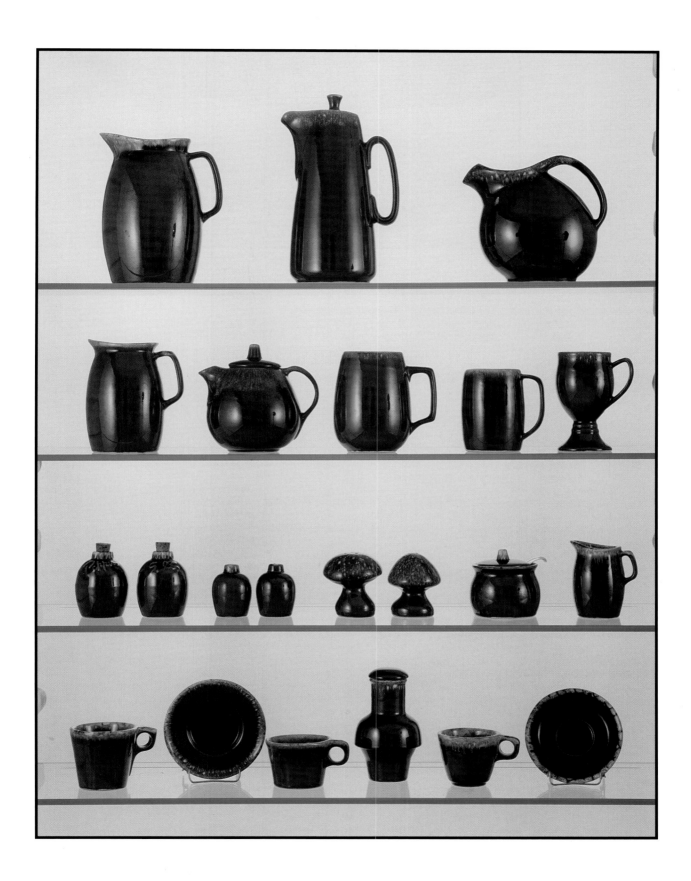

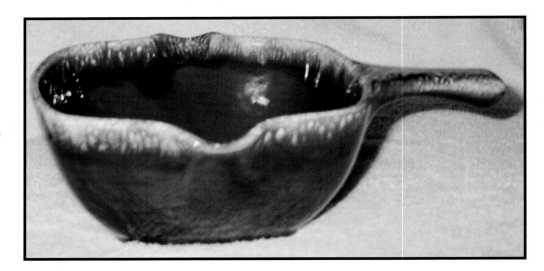

Rare Handled Server
#873H

Row 1:

    #5850   Casserole w/Chicken cover, 2 Qt.

    #560   Baker w/Chicken cover, 14⅜" L x 11" High (Rare)
                                 Inside Bottom of Roaster imprinted w/Rooster*

    #592   Hen on Nest Casserole, (Hard to Find)

Row 2:

    #508   Oval Salad, (Inside Bottom imprinted w/Rooster)*

    #523   Cookie Jar w/lid, 94 Oz.

    #594   Spoon Rest, 6¾" High x 4¾" Wide

Row 3:

    #510   Bean Pot, 2 Qt.

    #5280   Casserole w/Duck cover, 2 Pt.

    #540   Gravy Boat Set

Row 4:

    #196   Sitting Pig Bank

    #197   Jumbo Corky Pig Bank (Difficult to Find)

    #195   Corky Pig Bank

*This "Rooster" imprint was also used for an experimental dinnerware starter set. These pieces are extremely difficult to find and are highly prized by H&G dinnerware collectors.

In addition, two other much sought after experimental sets not shown in this book are decorated with a pie crust swirl design on the edge and another with an incised star decoration. Some examples of these pieces are represented in Brenda Robert's *The Collectors Encyclopedia of Hull Pottery* First Edition, page 153.

Bowls

Mixing Bowls are prized collector items. These pieces were often highly used and are difficult to find in a quality condition. Manufactured in lesser quantities than the fruit and salad bowls, the mixing bowls are more difficult to find.

Row 1:

#545	Salad Bowl, 10¼"
#852H	Mixing Bowl, 8¼" (Provincial Mold)
#850H	Mixing Bowl, 5¼" (Provincial Mold)
Not Shown:	#851H Mixing Bowl, 6¾" (Provincial Mold)

Row 2:   *Row 3:*

#538	Mixing Bowl, 8"		#569	Soup or Salad Bowl, 6½"
#537	Mixing Bowl, 7"		#503	Fruit/Cereal Bowl, 5¼"
#536	Mixing Bowl, 6"		#533	Fruit Bowl, 6"

Note: The bowls listed as Provincial molds are not shown in any of the following House 'n Gardens brochures in the mirror brown. However, these molds are featured in the Provincial line as well as the later Country Squire line. As collectors are quick to learn, pieces from one line can often be found glazed in colors from other lines. Short term productions and employee specials account for these special finds!

So count yourself fortunate to have come across such items, and merrily add them to your set. It adds more interest and value to your collection!

#853H Bake Dish Casserole
(Provincial Mold)

#545 Salad or Spaghetti Bowl
with #547 Fork & Spoon Set.

Row 1:

#524	Individual Bean Pot, 12 Oz.
#551	Not Shown: #524 w/slotted lid "Mustard or Jam Jar"
#585	Vinegar Server, 12 Oz. (Difficult to Find)
#582	Cheese Server 12 Oz. (Difficult to Find)
#584	Oil Server, 12 Oz. (Difficult to Find)
#576	Custard Cup, 6 Oz.

Row 2:

#581	Individual Oval Spaghetti Plate, (Marked "Spaghetti")
#561	Covered Butter Dish
#583	Rectangular Salad Server

Row 3:

#507	Casserole w/cover, 32 Oz. (Crestone Mold)*
#544	Oval Casserole w/lid
#574	Oval Serving Dish (Smaller size produced later) 10" x 5" x 1⅝"

Row 4:

#589	Bake 'n Serve, 6½"
#542	Divided Vegetable Dish, 10¾" x 7¼"
#553	Soup Mug, 11 Oz.
#554	Tray for Snack Set

*Note: This casserole can be found both with and without the Crestone imprint on the bottom. This mold, like the #599 Luncheon Plate was also carried over from the Crestone line and produced in the H&G line.

Now the fun really begins....The molds on the following pages represent some of the more interesting pieces in the House 'n Garden dinnerware line.

Row 1:

#595	Handled Skillet, 11½" x 7¾"
#527	French Handled Casserole w/cover *
#591	Deviled Egg Server w/Rooster imprint

Row 2:

#593	Oval Well 'n Tree Steak Plate, 14" x 10"
#541	Individual Steak Plate, 11¾" x 9"

Row 3:

#579	Covered French Handled Casserole w/warmer, 3 Pt. (Set very difficult to find, especially with the warmer!)
#565	Dutch Oven, 3 Pt. (Both top and bottom are from the same mold)
#566	Pie Plate, 9¼" (Difficult to Find)

This pie plate picture is compliments of Cindy Mountz. By some stroke of foresight, Cindy never removed the paper center!

* Note: This particular mold set was a very popular restaurant item. In fact, the molds were first leased to Western Stoneware of Illinois after the closing of the factory in 1985 and finally all rights were sold to Western Stoneware several years later. These pieces are still in manufacture and can often be found in use at many restaurants throughout the U.S. today!

Row 1:

#584	Sauce Bowl for Chip 'n Dip Set (Rare)
#585	Tray for Chip 'n Dip Set (Rare)
#563	Ash Tray, 8" w/Deer imprint

Row 2:

#591	Leaf Shaped Chip 'n Dip, 12¼" x 9"
#590	Individual Leaf Dish, 7¼" x 4¾"
#583	Chip 'n Dip (Very Rare)

Row 3:

#573	Corn Serving Dish (Difficult to Find)
#521	Leaf Shaped Chip 'n Dip, 15" x 10½"
#870H	Bud Vase, 9" (Difficult to Find)
Below: #596	Fish Platter (Rare)

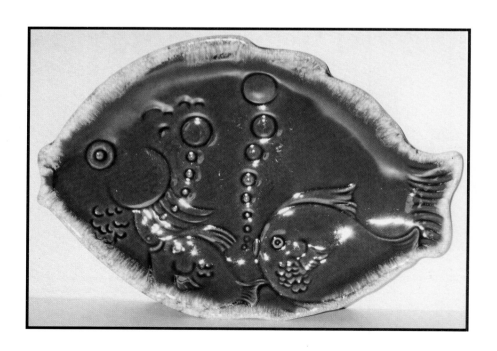

Photo courtesy of Cindy Mountz of Elverson, PA.

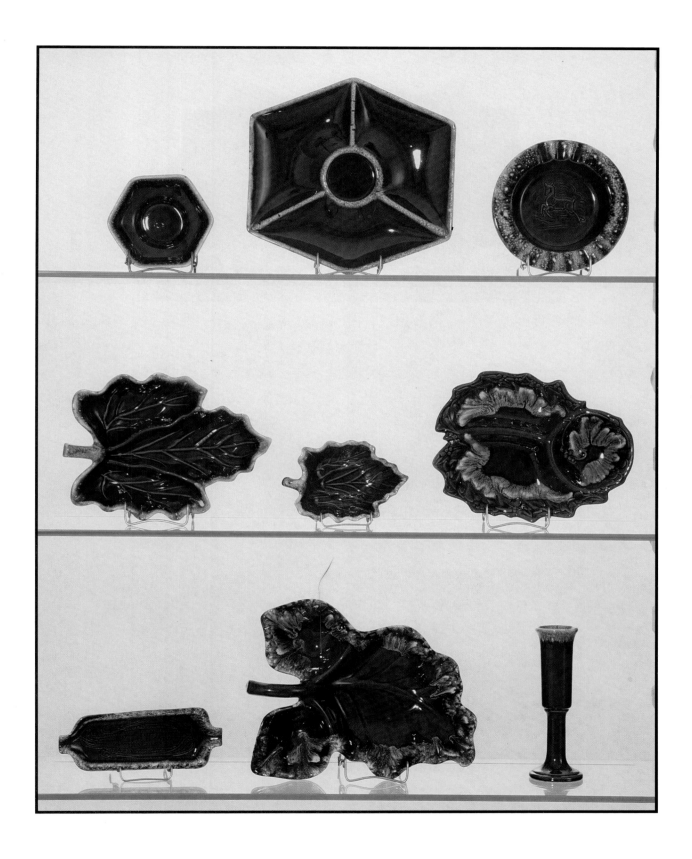

#577   Double Serving Dish (Rare) (Top View)

ONLY SHOWN IN BROCHURES:

These pieces are not, unfortunately a part of my collection, but are the only items I am missing from this dinnerware line. They are shown in the following brochure pages.

   #535   Roaster w/cover (Difficult to Find)

   #557   Oval Platter w/Rooster imprint (Rare)

   #556-557-558-559 Canister Set (Round), Tea, Coffee, Sugar and Flour
                   (Difficult to Find Undamaged)

The following pages contain brochures and price lists from the late 60's. I have included the price lists to provide information on wholesale prices at the time the pottery was manufactured. So don't write to Hull Pottery to place your order....we only wish we could!

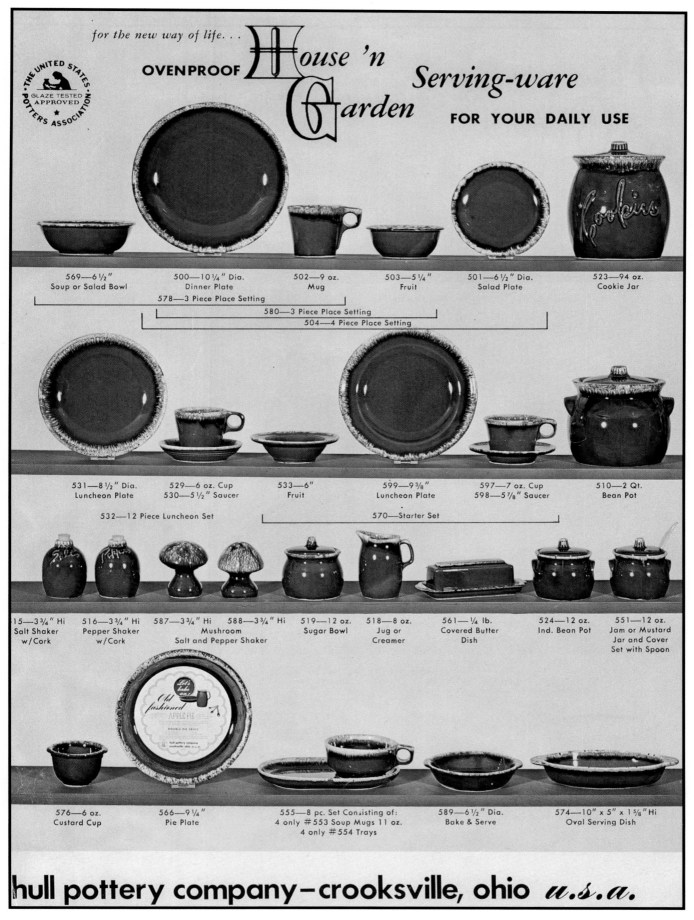

for the new way of life...

OVENPROOF House 'n Garden Serving-ware

FOR YOUR DAILY USE

THE UNITED STATES · POTTERS ASSOCIATION · GLAZE TESTED APPROVED

569—6½"
Soup or Salad Bowl

500—10¼" Dia.
Dinner Plate

502—9 oz.
Mug

503—5¼"
Fruit

501—6½" Dia.
Salad Plate

523—94 oz.
Cookie Jar

578—3 Piece Place Setting

580—3 Piece Place Setting

504—4 Piece Place Setting

531—8½" Dia.
Luncheon Plate

529—6 oz. Cup
530—5½" Saucer

533—6"
Fruit

599—9⅜"
Luncheon Plate

597—7 oz. Cup
598—5⅞" Saucer

510—2 Qt.
Bean Pot

532—12 Piece Luncheon Set

570—Starter Set

15—3¾" Hi
Salt Shaker
w/Cork

516—3¾" Hi
Pepper Shaker
w/Cork

587—3¾" Hi
588—3¾" Hi
Mushroom
Salt and Pepper Shaker

519—12 oz.
Sugar Bowl

518—8 oz.
Jug or
Creamer

561—¼ lb.
Covered Butter
Dish

524—12 oz.
Ind. Bean Pot

551—12 oz.
Jam or Mustard
Jar and Cover
Set with Spoon

576—6 oz.
Custard Cup

566—9¼"
Pie Plate

555—8 pc. Set Consisting of:
4 only #553 Soup Mugs 11 oz.
4 only #554 Trays

589—6½" Dia.
Bake & Serve

574—10" x 5" x 1⅝" Hi
Oval Serving Dish

hull pottery company—crooksville, ohio u.s.a.

House 'n Garden Serving-ware by Hull

526—16 oz.
Beer Stein

571—10 oz.
Continental Mug

592
Hen on Nest Casserole

5280—2 Pt.
Casserole w/Duck Cover

5770—2 Qt.
Casserole w/Duck Cover

5850—2 Qt.
Casserole w/Chicken Cover

5840—2 Pt.
Casserole w/Chicken Cover

542—10¾" x 7¼"
Divided Vegetable

540 Gravy Boat Set
Consisting of 1 each 511 and 512

196 Sitting
Piggy Bank

195 Corky
Piggy Bank

197 Jumbo Corky
Piggy Bank

545—10¼" Salad
or Spaghetti Bowl

547—Fork and Spoon Set
546—3 Piece Salad Set Consisting of:
1 only #545—Salad Bowl
1 only #547—Fork and Spoon Set

593—14" x 10"
Oval Well 'n Tree
Steak Plate

541—11¾" x 9"
Ind. Oval Steak Plate

565—3 Pt. Dutch Oven
Consists of two only
568—3 Pt. Square Baker

544—10" x 7¼" (2 Pt.)
Oval Casserole
w/Cover
543—10" x 7¼" (2 Pt.)
Oval Baker Open

548—10" x 7¼" (2 Qt.)
Oval Casserole

THE UNITED STATES
POTTERS ASSOCIATION
GLAZE TESTED
APPROVED

28

Mirror Brown trimmed in Ivory Foam

514—2 Qt.
Ice Jug

525—2 Pt.
Jug

509—5 Pt.
Jug

522—8 Cup
Coffee Pot

507—32 oz.
Casserole w/Cover
506—32 oz. Casserole Open

536—6"
Mixing Bowl

537—7"
Mixing Bowl

538—8"
Mixing Bowl
w/Pouring Spout

539—3 Pc. Mixing Bowl Set
(6", 7", 8")

Discontinued

Discontinued

527—5¼"
French Handled Casserole
with Cover

513 French Handled
Casserole Open

521—15" x 10½"
Leaf Shaped
Chip 'n Dip

563—8" Dia.
Ash Tray

549—5 Cup
Tea Pot

hull pottery company—crooksville, ohio *u.s.a.*

502—4 Coffee Mug 9 oz.
4 Piece Party Pack Set
(Individual Carton—12 sets to Master)

526—4 Beer Stein 16 oz.
4 Piece Party Pack Set
(Individual Carton—6 sets to Master)

570 OVENPROOF 16 PIECE STARTER SET

4—Fruits - 6"
4—Cups - 7 oz.
4—Saucers - 5⅞"
4—Plates - 9⅜"

504 OVENPROOF 16 PIECE STARTER SET

4—Fruits - 5¼"   4—Salad Plates - 6½"
4—Mugs - 9 oz.   4—Dinner Plates - 10¼" Dia.

hull pottery company—crooksville, ohio *u.s.a.*

for the new way of life . . .

OVENPROOF *House 'n Garden Serving-ware*

FOR YOUR DAILY NEEDS

569 6½" Soup or Salad Bowl	**500 Dinner Plate** 10¼" Dia.	**502 Mug** 9 oz.	**503 Fruit** 5¼"	**501 Salad Plate** 6½" Dia.	**523 Cookie Jar** w/cover 94 oz.

578—3 PIECE PLACE SETTING

580—3 PIECE PLACE SETTING

504—4 PIECE PLACE SETTING

509 Water Jug 5 pint	**525 Jug** 2 pt.	**518 Jug or Creamer** 8 oz.	**519 Sugar Bowl** w/cover 12 oz.	**510 Bean Pot** w/cover 2 qt.	**524 Individual Bean Pot w/cover** 12 oz.	**522 Coffee Pot** w/cover 8 cup

527 French Handled Casserole w/cover 5¼"	**514 Ice Jug** 2 qt.	**515 Salt Shaker** w/cork 3¾" Hi.	**516 Pepper Shaker** w/cork 3¾" Hi.	**521 Leaf Shaped Chip 'n Dip** 15" x 10½"	**526 Beer Stein** 16 oz.

 hull pottery company — crooksville, ohio *u.s.a.*

Mirror Brown trimmed in Ivory Foam

DISCONTINUED

541
Individual Oval Steak Plate
11¾" x 9"

542
Divided Vegetable
10¾" x 7¼"

544
Oval Casserole w/Cover
10" x 7¼" (2 pt.)

545—Salad or Spaghetti Bowl 10¼"   547—Fork and Spoon Set
546—Three piece Salad Set consisting of:
1 only #545—Salad Bowl
1 only #547—Fork & Spoon Set

548
Oval Casserole w/Cover
2 qt.—10" x 7¼"

549
Tea Pot & Cover
5 cup

551
Jam or Mustard Jar & Cover
Set with Spoon
12 oz.

561
Covered Butter Dish
¼ lb. capacity

563
Ash Tray
8" Dia.

566
Pie Plate
9¼" Dia.

555—8 pc. Set Consisting of:
4 only #553 Soup Mugs 11 oz.
4 only #554 Trays

579
Covered French Handled
Casserole w/Warmer
3 pt.

565
Dutch Oven
3 pt.

32

*New Addition to Hull's Famous Ovenproof**

House 'n Garden Serving-ware

529 Cup - 6 oz.
530 Saucer - 5½"
531 Luncheon Plate - 8½" Dia.

532 — 12 Piece Luncheon Set

4—Cups - 6 oz.
4—Saucers - 5½"
4—Luncheon Plates - 8½" Dia.

536 Mixing Bowl
6"

537 Mixing Bowl
7"

538 Mixing Bowl
w/Pouring Spout 8"

539—3 Pc. Mixing Bowl Set
(6", 7", 8")

*572 Jumbo Stein
32 oz.

*574 Oval Serving Dish
10" x 5" x 1⅝"

590 Ind. Leaf Dish
7¼" x 4¾"

591 Leaf Shaped Chip'n Dip
12¼" x 9"

* 592 Hen on Nest Casserole

*195 Corky Piggy Bank
Mirror Brown
Trimmed in Blue

*195 Corky Piggy Bank
Mirror Brown
Trimmed in Pink

*196 Sitting Piggy Bank
Mirror Brown Trimmed
in Yellow & Turquoise

*197 Jumbo Corky
Piggy Bank
Mirror Brown Trimmed
in Yellow & Turquoise

Mirror Brown trimmed in Ivory Foam

566 Pie Plate
9 ¼ "

**"The Nation's number one line
for casual living —
The new and fashionable way
of life"**

502-4 Coffee Mug - 9 oz.
4 Piece Party Pack Set
(Individual carton — 12 sets to master)

504 OVENPROOF 16 PIECE STARTER SET

4—Fruits - 5 ¼ "   4—Salad Plates - 6 ½ "
4—Mugs - 9 oz.   4—Dinner Plates - 10 ¼ " Dia.

**New Addition to Hull's
Famous Ovenproof**

House 'n Garden *Serving-ware*

508 Oval Salad   571 Continental Mug   576 Custard Cup   573 Corn Serving Dish   583 Chip 'n Dip

577 Double Serving Dish   584 Sauce Bowl   585 Tray   586 Chip 'n Dip (2 pc. Set)

512 Gravy Boat Saucer   511 Gravy Boat   540 Gravy Boat Set   534 Open Roaster   535 Roaster w/cover

557 Chicken Platter
13 3/8" x 10 1/2" x 2"

559 Covered Platter

558 Open Chicken Baker
13 3/8" x 10 1/2" x 3"

560 Covered Roaster
556 Chicken Top Replacement

575 Chicken Top, Platter and Baker Set

hull pottery company — crooksville, ohio *u.s.a.*

35

Additions to Hull's Famous Ovenproof

House 'n Garden

Serving-Ware

505 Carafe w/cover (2 cup)

506 Open Baker 32 oz.

507 Casserole w/cover 32 oz.

528 4 pc. Coffee Carafe Set

consisting of
1 only Coffee Carafe w/c
1 only Coffee Cup 7 oz.
1 only Deep Well Saucer

594 Table Size Salt Shaker
595 Table Size Pepper Shaker
596 Table Size Salt & Pepper Set

533 Fruit 6"

593 Oval Well 'n Tree Steak Plate 14" x 10"

hull pottery company crooksville, ohio *u.s.a.*

HULL POTTERY CROOKSVILLE, OHIO

597 Cup 7 oz.

598 Saucer 5 7/8"

599 Luncheon Plate 9 3/8"

Look at the angle of this. Our extra deep wells in the saucers will save many spills.

One outstanding feature also in the design is that it permits easy stacking that takes less storage area.

570 — Ovenproof 16 Piece Starter Set

4—Fruits 6"
4—Cups 7 oz.
4—Saucers 5 7/8"
4—Plates 9 3/8"

Mirror Brown trimmed in Ivory Foam

Additions to the nation's #1 line for casual living

House 'n Garden Serving-ware

THE UNITED STATES
GLAZE TESTED
APPROVED
POTTERS ASSOCIATION

591—9¼"

595
11½" × 7¾" × 1¾"

594
6¾" × 4¾"

596
11¼" × 7¾"

Canisters

556
5½" × 5½"

557
6⅞" × 6¾"

558
7⅞" × 8"

559
9" × 9¼"

The nation's number one line for casual living offers these new creations.

This newly designed canister set is available in four sizes.

The flour and sugar canisters each have a liberal capacity of five pounds, the most commonly purchased package size. Since coffee and tea are available, either bulk or packaged, capacity is not indicated.

No homemaker's kitchen is complete without the spoon rest and the handled serving dish.

Much thought has been given to every detail and purpose of the **individual** fish platter and handled serving dish.

Our deviled egg server takes less space on your table yet holds one/half dozen eggs. You will never worry about them rolling off with our specially shaped wells.

HULL POTTERY

hull pottery company—crooksville, ohio *u.s.a.*

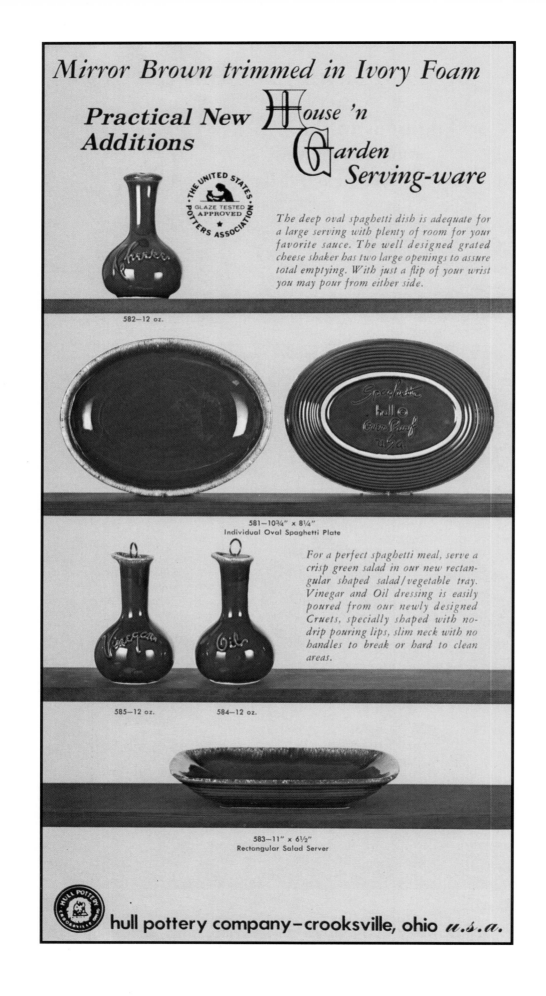

Mirror Brown trimmed in Ivory Foam

Practical New Additions

House 'n Garden Serving-ware

The deep oval spaghetti dish is adequate for a large serving with plenty of room for your favorite sauce. The well designed grated cheese shaker has two large openings to assure total emptying. With just a flip of your wrist you may pour from either side.

582—12 oz.

581—10¾" x 8¼"
Individual Oval Spaghetti Plate

For a perfect spaghetti meal, serve a crisp green salad in our new rectangular shaped salad/vegetable tray. Vinegar and Oil dressing is easily poured from our newly designed Cruets, specially shaped with no-drip pouring lips, slim neck with no handles to break or hard to clean areas.

585—12 oz.   584—12 oz.

583—11" x 6½"
Rectangular Salad Server

hull pottery company—crooksville, ohio u.s.a.

Hull Pottery Co., Crooksville, Ohio 43731

NEW HOUSE 'N GARDEN ITEMS
Mirror Brown trimmed in Ivory Foam

July 14, 1969

OVENPROOF

ITEM NO.	DESCRIPTION	PACKED	APPROX. WEIGHT	PRICE DOZEN
508	Oval Chicken Salad 6-1/2" x 5-1/4"	2 doz.	22 lb.	$ 3.00
511	Gravy Boat 16 oz.	1 doz.	18 lb.	12.00
512	Gravy Boat Saucer 10-1/4" x 6"	1 doz.	17 lb.	7.20
540	Gravy Boat Set—consisting of: 1 each 511-512	6 sets	17 lb.	1.60 set
534	Roaster (open) 7 pt.	1/3 doz.	15 lb.	16.20
535	Roaster w/cover 7 pt.	1/3 doz.	25 lb.	24.00
535-1	Roaster w/cover (Individually packed in reshipper carton)	1 only	7 lb.	2.50 each
556	Chicken Cover (replacement cost)	1 only	6 lb.	2.40 each
557	Chicken Server 13-3/8" x 10-1/2" x 2"	1/2 doz.	21 lb.	15.00
558	Open Chicken Baker 13-3/8" x 10-1/2" x 3"	1/3 doz.	16 lb.	17.28
559	Server w/Chicken Cover 13-3/8" L. x 10 " Hi.	1 only	11 lb.	3.65 each
560	Baker w/Chicken Cover 13-3/8" L. x 11" Hi.	1 only	11-1/2 lb.	3.75 each
575	Chicken Cover, Server and Baker Set consisting of: 556-557-558	1 set	14 lb.	5.00 set
571	Continental Mug 10 oz.	1 doz.	15 lb.	6.60
573	Corn Serving Dish 9-1/4" x 3-3/8"	2 doz.	22 lb.	4.20
576	Custard Cup 6 oz.	4 doz.	21 lb.	2.28
577	Double Serving Dish 14-1/2" x 8-1/2"	1/3 doz.	15 lb.	19.20
583	Chip 'n Dip 11-1/2" x 8-3/4"	1/2 doz.	15 lb.	13.20
584	Sauce Bowl 5-1/2" dia.	2 doz.	21 lb.	3.00
585	Tray 12" x 11"	2/3 doz.	24 lb.	18.00
586	Chip 'n Dip (2 pc. set) consisting of: 1 each 584-585	6 sets	23 lb.	1.80 set

Mirror Brown House 'n Garden—continued

ITEM NO.	DESCRIPTION	PACKED	APPROX. WEIGHT	PRICE DOZEN
574	Oval Serving Dish 10" x 5" x 1-5/8" Hi.	2 doz.	28 lb.	$ 6.96
578	12 Pc. Serving-ware Set consisting of: . . . . 4 only 500 Dinner Plates 10-1/2" dia. . . . . 4 only 502—9 oz. Mugs 4 only 569 Soup or Salad 6-1/2" dia.	1 set	17 lb.	4.73 set
579	French Hdld. Casserole w/cover & warmer	1 set	6-1/2 lb.	2.52 set
580	12 Pc. Serving-ware Set consisting of: . . . . 4 only 500 Dinner Plates 10-1/4" dia. 4 only 502—9 oz. Mugs 4 only 503 Fruits 5-1/2" dia.	1 set	15 lb.	4.20 set
590	Individual Leaf Dish 7-1/4" x 4-3/4"	2 doz.	18 lb.	4.68
591	Leaf Shaped Chip 'n Dip 12-1/4" x 9" . . . . .1/2 doz.	1/2 doz.	15 lb.	13.80
592	Hen on Nest Casserole . . . . .1/2 doz.	1/2 doz.	25 lb.	20.16
593	Oval Well 'n Tree Steak Plate 14" x 10" . . . . .1/2 doz.	1/2 doz.	18 lb.	15.12
594	Table size Salt Shaker	2 doz.	9 lb.	3.24
595	Table size Pepper Shaker	2 doz.	9 lb.	3.24
596	Table size Salt & Pepper Set	12 sets	9 lb.	.55 set
597	Cup 7 oz.	4 doz.	27 lb.	3.24
598	Saucer 5-7/8"	2 doz.	14 lb.	2.52
599	Luncheon Plate 9-3/8"	1 doz.	19 lb.	6.12
1095	45 Piece Dinner Set consisting of: . . . . 8 only 500 Dinner Plate 10-1/4" 8 only 501 Salad Plate 6-1/2" 8 only 503 Fruit 5-1/4" 8 only 529 Cup 6 oz. 8 only 530 Saucer 5-1/2" 1 only 520 Sugar & Creamer Set 1 only 541 Steak Plate 11-3/4" x 9" 1 only 542 Divided Vegetable Dish 10-3/4" x 7-1/4"	1 set	43 lb.	13.76 set

HAND DECORATED PIGGY BANKS

195	Corky Piggy Bank . . . . Color: Mirror Brown trimmed in Pink Mirror Brown trimmed in Blue	2 doz.	42 lb.	9.00
196	Sitting Piggy Bank . . . . Color: Mirror Brown trimmed in Yellow and Turquoise	2 doz.	42 lb.	9.00

NOTE: #195 and # 196 Corky Piggy Banks may be assorted in a 2 dozen carton

197	Jumbo Corky Piggy Bank . . . . .1/2 doz. Color: Mirror Brown trimmed in Yellow and Turquoise	1/2 doz.	20 lb.	21.00

"TERMS OF SALE"

Sold only in standard packages—no extra packing charge

Terms: 1% 15 days net 30—fob Crooksville, Ohio

NO ALLOWANCE FOR BREAKAGE—CLAIMS MUST BE FILED WITH COMMON CARRIER

see 600 SERIES LIST FOR ITEMS AVAILABLE IN "AVOCADO"

Items listed in both Mirror Brown and Avocado may be assorted in cartons at no extra cost.

HOUSE 'N GARDEN SERVING-WARE
Mirror Brown, trimmed in Ivory Foam
OVENPROOF

"the nation's number one line for casual living— the new and fashionable way of life"

ITEM NO.	DESCRIPTION	PACKED	APPROX. WEIGHT	PRICE DOZEN
500	Dinner Plate 10-1/4" Dia.	1 doz.	24 lb.	$ 6.96
501	Salad Plate 6-1/2" Dia.	2 doz.	18 lb.	2.52
502	Mug 9 oz.	4 doz.	40 lb.	3.36
502-4	Coffee Mug 9 oz. 4 Piece Party Pack Set (Individual carton—12 sets to master)	12 sets	40 lb.	1.22 set
503	Fruit 5-1/4"	2 doz.	21 lb.	2.52
504	Starter Set consisting of: 4 only 500 Dinner Plate 10-1/4" 4 only 501 Salad Plate 6-1/2" 4 only 502 Mug 9 oz. 4 only 503 Fruit 5-1/4"	1 set	17 lb.	4.83 set
505	Carafe w/cover 2 cup	1 doz.	14 lb.	6.96
506	Open Baker 32 oz.	1 doz.	21 lb.	6.84
507	Casserole w/cover 32 oz.	1 doz.	30 lb.	8.64
509	Water Jug 5 pt. (old fashioned)	1/2 doz.	22 lb.	12.60
510	Bean Pot w/cover 2 qt.	1/2 doz.	21 lb.	12.60
513	French Handled Casserole 12 oz.	2 doz.	21 lb.	3.36
514	Ice Jug 2 qt.	1/2 doz.	17 lb.	11.40
515	Salt Shaker w/cork 3-3/4" Hi.	2 doz.	15 lb.	3.72
516	Pepper Shaker w/cork 3-3/4" Hi.	2 doz.	15 lb.	3.72
517	Salt & Pepper Set	12 sets	15 lb.	.63 set
518	Creamer	2 doz.	18 lb.	3.24
519	Sugar Bowl w/cover 12 oz.	2 doz.	21 lb.	4.56
520	Sugar & Creamer Set	12 sets	20 lb.	.65 set
521	Leaf Shaped Chip 'n Dip	1/3 doz.	13 lb.	20.16
522	Coffee Pot w/cover 8 cup	1/2 doz.	20 lb.	20.16
523	Cookie Jar w/cover 94 oz.	1/2 doz.	23 lb.	15.96
524	Individual Bean Pot w/cover 12 oz.	2 doz.	21 lb.	4.56
525	Jug 2 pt.	1 doz.	21 lb.	6.96
526	Beer Stein 16 oz.	2 doz.	28 lb.	4.80
526-4	Beer Stein 16 oz. 4 Piece Party Pack Set (Individual carton—6 sets to master)	6 sets	30 lb.	1.79 set
527	Covered French Hdld. Casserole 12 oz. (same as 513 except with cover)	2 doz.	33 lb.	4.32
528	4 Pc. Coffee Carafe Set—consisting of: 1 only 505 Coffee Carafe w/cover 1 only 597 Coffee Cup 7 oz. 1 only 598 Saucer 5-7/8"	1 set	3 lb.	1.22 set
529	Cup 6 oz.	4 doz.	32 lb.	3.24

"Terms of Sale" appear at bottom of page 3

Mirror Brown House 'n Garden—continued

ITEM NO.	DESCRIPTION	PACKED	APPROX. WEIGHT	PRICE DOZEN
530	Saucer 5-1/2"	2 doz.	17 lb.	$ 2.52
531	Plate 8-1/2"	1 doz.	17 lb.	5.52
532	12 Pc. Luncheon Set—consisting of:	1 set	13 lb.	3.62 set
	4 only 529 Cups 6 oz.			
	4 only 530 Saucers 5-1/2"			
	4 only 531 Luncheon Plates 8-1/2"			
533	Fruit 6"	2 doz.	21 lb.	3.12
536	Mixing Bowl 6"	3 doz.	41 lb.	3.60
537	Mixing Bowl 7"	2 doz.	41 lb.	4.68
538	Mixing Bowl w/Pouring Spout 8"	1 doz.	29 lb.	5.64
539	3 Pc. Mixing Bowl Set (6", 7", 8")	6 sets	31 lb.	1.26 set
541	Individual Oval Steak Plate 11-3/4" x 9"	1 doz.	27 lb.	7.56
542	Divided Vegetable Dish 10-3/4" x 7-1/4"	1/2 doz.	15 lb.	10.08
543	Oval Baker 10" x 7-1/4"	1/2 doz.	13 lb.	8.04
544	Oval Casserole w/cover 2 pt.	1/2 doz.	21 lb.	11.76
545	Salad or Spaghetti Bowl 10-1/4"	1/3 doz.	13 lb.	12.00
546	3 Pc. Salad Set—Consisting of:	4 sets	13 lb.	1.26 set
	1 only 545 Salad Bowl 10-1/4"			
	1 only 547—Fork & Spoon Set			
547	Fork and Spoon Set	12 sets	2 lb.	.42 set
548	Deep Oval Casserole and cover 2 qt.	1/3 doz.	17 lb.	15.96
549	Tea Pot and cover 5 cup	1/2 doz.	14 lb.	10.08
550	Jam or Mustard Jar and cover 12 oz.	2 doz.	21 lb.	4.56
551	Jam or Mustard Jar and Cover Set consisting of:	24 sets	21 lb.	.48 set
	1 only 550—Jam or Mustard Jar and Cover			
	1 only 552—Crystal Plastic Spoon			
552	Jam or Mustard Spoon/Crystal Plastic	2 doz.	1/2 lb.	1.47
553	Soup Mug 11 oz.	2 doz.	23 lb.	4.08
554	Tray 9-1/2" x 5-3/4"	2 doz.	27 lb.	5.64
555	8 Pc. Soup 'n Sandwich Set consisting of:	1 set	8 lb.	3.34 set
	4 only 553 Soup Mugs 11 oz.			
	4 only 554 Trays			
561	Covered Butter Dish (1/4 lb. capacity)	1 doz.	18 lb.	7.32
562	3 Pt. Covered French Hdld. Casserole	1/3 doz.	18 lb.	13.80
563	Ash Tray 8" dia.	1 doz.	18 lb.	6.36
564	Candle Flame Warmer & Candle	1/2 doz.	11 lb.	8.40
565	Dutch Oven 8-3/4" x 9-1/2" x 2-1/2"—consists of :	1/2 doz.	30 lb.	17.04
	(2 only 568 Square Bakers)			
566	Pie Plate 9-1/4" dia.	1 doz.	24 lb.	6.96
567	Open French Hdld. Casserole 3 pt.	1/3 doz.	12 lb.	10.08
568	Square Baker 3 pt.	1 doz.	30 lb.	8.52
569	6-1/2" Soup or Salad Bowl	2 doz.	29 lb.	4.56
570	Starter Set consisting of:	1 set	15 lb.	4.73 set
	4 only 533 Fruits 6"			
	4 only 597 Cups 7 oz.			
	4 only 598 Saucers 5-7/8"			
	4 only 599 Plates 9-3/8"			
572	Jumbo Stein 32 oz.	1 doz.	25 lb.	7.32

"Terms of Sale" appear at bottom of page 3

Hull Pottery Co., Crooksville, Ohio 43731

HOUSE 'N GARDEN SERVING-WARE
Mirror Brown trimmed in Ivory Foam

July 14, 1969

OVENPROOF

#6036—86 Piece Introductory Assortment Featuring New Items

QUANTITY ASSORTMENT	DESCRIPTION	APPROX. WEIGHT	PRICE DOZEN	PRICE ASST.
1/3 doz.	535 Roaster w/Cover 7 pt.	25 lbs.	$24.00	$ 8.00
4 only	540 Gravy Boat Set . . . . consisting of: 1 each: 511-512	12 lbs.	1.60 set	6.40
2 only	559 Server w/Chicken Cover . . . . 13-3/8" L. x 10" Hi.	22 lbs.	3.65 each	7.30
2 only	560 Baker w/Chicken Cover . . . . 13-3/8" L. x 11" Hi.	23 lbs.	3.75 each	7.50
1 doz.	571 Continental Mug 10 oz.	15 lbs.	6.60	6.60
1 doz.	573 Corn Serving Dish . . . . 9-1/4" x 3-3/8"	11 lbs.	4.20	4.20
2 doz.	576 Custard Cup 6 oz.	10 lbs.	2.28	4.56
1/3 doz.	577 Double Serving Dish 14-1/2" x 8-1/2"	15 lbs.	19.20	6.40
1/6 doz.	583 Chip 'n Dip 11-1/2" x 8-3/4"	5 lbs.	13.20	2.20
4 only	586 Chip 'n Dip (2 pc. set) . . . . consisting of: 1 each: 584-585	15 lbs.	1.80 set	7.20

86 Pieces (Including covers)

$60.36

Approximate weight — 153 lbs.

Terms: 1% 15 days net 30 — fob Crooksville, Ohio

PROVINCIAL

Provincial serving ware was a short-lived dual glazed dinnerware line. With the exception of the #705, #706, #707 mixing bowls and the #711 bake dish*, the House 'n Garden molds were used to produce this unusual and difficult to manufacture line. The piece was first glazed in white, then finished by dipping in the mirror brown to cover the bottoms, leaving the tops and insides white. Obviously, the most difficult pieces to finish were the dinner plates and the salad plates.

Due to the extremely difficult finish, the line was discontinued shortly after it had begun. Thus, these pieces are extremely rare and difficult to find. Due to the nature of the finish, this line does not lend itself to everyday use, however they are still prized pieces to acquire for Hull dinnerware collectors, simply because they are so unusual and rare.

Picture 1:

#700	Dinner Plate, 10¼"
#724	Individual Bean Pot, 12 Oz.
#702	Mug, 9 Oz.
#702P	Saucer
#718	Creamer, 8 Oz.
#706	Mixing Bowl, 6¾"

Picture 2: #723   Cookie Jar

Picture 3: #710   Bean Pot w/cover, 2 Qt.

Other items not shown:

#701	Salad Plate, 6½"
#703	Fruit Bowl, 5¼"
#722	Coffee Pot, 60 Oz., (Warmer Very Rare)
#705	Mixing Bowl, 5¼"
#707	Mixing Bowl, 8¼"
#709	Water Jug, 5 Pt.
#725	Jug, 2 Pt.
#719	Sugar Bowl
#711	Bake Dish, 3 Pt., (Warmer Very Rare)
#713	French Handled Casserole, 5¼"
#726	Beer Stein, 16 Oz.
#714	Ice Jug, 2 Pt.
#715	Salt Shaker, 3¾"
#716	Pepper Shaker, 3¾"
#721	Chip 'n Dip, 15" x 10½", (Most Common Piece)

*Note: The mixing bowl and bake dish molds are represented in the Country Squire brochures as #105, #106, #107 and #112.

Photos courtesy of Lori Friend of Statesville, North Carolina.

PICTURE 1:

PICTURE 2:

PICTURE 3:

RAINBOW

One of the most colorful lines, Rainbow consisted of the original mirror brown, tangerine, green agate and butterscotch glazes offered in a starter set with several companion accessories. This line spawned the green agate Country Squire and Tangerine as covered in the following sections, making it difficult to separate the various lines.

Row 1:

#122	Coffee Pot, (Country Squire)
#232RA	Coffee Cup, 6 Oz. Butterscotch
#233RA	Saucer, 5½" Butterscotch
#232RA	Coffee Cup, 6 Oz. Green Agate

Row 2:

#235RA	Salad Plate, 6½" Butterscotch
#538	Mixing Bowl, 8" Tangerine
#101	Salad Plate, 6½" (Country Squire)

Row 3:

#115&6	Salt & Pepper (Country Squire)
#540	Serv-All Leaf Tray, 12" x 7½" (Rare)
#103	Fruit Bowl (Country Squire)

No factory number was assigned to the individual glazes, thus each mold carries the same number. The pieces from this line were incorporated into the Country Squire and Tangerine lines. Also, the H&G pieces were included in this line, making distinction of the individual pieces difficult. Note: The House 'n Garden pieces are not listed under Rainbow in the index, but are shown here as they were a part of this dinnerware line.

Note: I apologize for any confusion by including the Country Squire pieces in this plate picture, however, it was not practical to separate these few items due to the small quantity of Country Squire in my collection.

If no color was specified when ordering,
the orders for Rainbow were filled with the mirror brown H&G pieces.

Row 1:

    #153   Soup Mug, 11 Oz. (Country Squire)

    #154   Snack Tray (Country Squire)

    #592   Two Tier Tidbit Tray Set

    #861RA   Soup Mug, 11 Oz. (Butterscotch)

    #862RA   Snack Tray (Butterscotch)

Row 2:

    #591   Leaf Shape Chip 'n Dip, (Butterscotch)

    #260RA   Mug, 9 Oz. (Green Agate)

    #260RA   Mug, 9 Oz. (Butterscotch)

    #591   Leaf Shape Chip 'n Dip (Tangerine)

Row 3:

    #590   Individual Leaf Dish (Tangerine)

    #261RA   Dinner Plate, 10½"
                       (Note the extra wide foam trim.)

    #590   Individual Leaf Dish (Green Agate)

Because the butterscotch glaze was not incorporated into any other line, and its only production was during the manufacture of the Rainbow line, this color is very difficult to find. While it is a nice addition to any Rainbow collection, few collectors have attempted to put together a set of the butterscotch pieces.

Rainbow snack set...what a colorful way to serve soup & sandwiches!

#540   Serv-All Leaf Tray, 12" x 7½" (Rare)

The mirror brown is just as difficult to find as any of the other Rainbow colors!

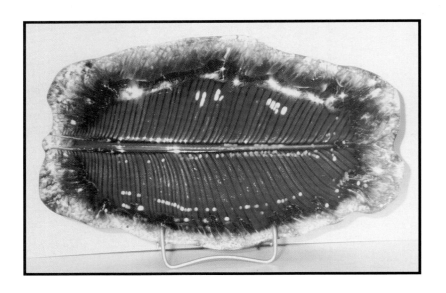

#123 Green Agate cookie jar with Tangerine Lid. Combinations like these were typical of the Rainbow line.

#592 The two-tiered tidbit was introduced in the Rainbow line but is considered a part of House 'n Garden series.

OVENPROOF RAINBOW LUNCHEON SET

#232—12 pc.
Plate 8½"
Cup 6 oz.
Saucer 5½"

by Hull

LUNCHEON SET
Illustrated

| Mirror Brown | Butterscotch | Green Agate | Tangerine |

Complete set also available in choice of each color shown—see list.

Also available in the four colors shown above.

No. 590 Individual
Leaf Dish 7¼" x 4¾"

No. 591 Leaf Shape
Chip 'n Dip 12¼" x 9"

Discontinued

*Here is a new Mixing Bowl Set added
to Hull's Famous line of House 'n Garden
Serving and Kitchen Ware*

No. 539—3 pc.
Mixing Bowl Set
(6"—7"—8")
Mirror Brown only

No. 538 Mixing
Bowl w/Pouring
Spout 8"

No. 537
Mixing Bowl 7"

No. 536
Mixing Bowl 6"

*Mixing Bowls and Serv-all Trays sold only
in Mirror Brown.*

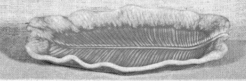

Discontinued

The complete line of House 'n Garden is available in Mirror Brown trimmed in Ivory Foam . . . See list for other items also offered in "Rainbow" assorted colors.

hull pottery company — crooksville, ohio *u.s.a.*

TANGERINE

An offspring of the Rainbow line, the tangerine glaze was marketed as House 'n Garden serving ware. No other title was given to the line. The molds were all from the H&G line with no new designs added. This bold bright glaze is very attractive to collectors, but the pieces are difficult to find. Generally, the prices run 25% or more higher for Tangerine, than for the H&G mirror brown.

This line is one of my favorites because of its colorful glaze, and I eagerly search for additions to this line for my collection.

Row 1:

#942	Divided Vegetable, 10¾" x 7¼"
#901	Salad Plate, 6½"
#902	Coffee Mug, 9 Oz.
#926	Beer Stein, 16 Oz.

Row 2:

#965	Dutch Oven, 3 Pt. (Both the top and bottom are from the same mold)
#969	Soup or Salad Bowl, 6½"
#945	Spaghetti Bowl, 10¼"

Row 3:

#941	Individual Steak Plate, 11¾" x 9"
#966	Pie Plate, 9¼"
#900	Dinner Plate, 10¼"

Many pieces can be added to your collection from the Rainbow and Imperial lines to make it more interesting and fun. Mixing the pieces with those from the Avocado line is also very attractive. In fact, many of the Imperial centerpieces that are glazed in tangerine have a green foam trim, such as the #F71 Swan Planter shown on page 113.

Row 1:

#953	Soup Mug, 11 Oz.
#954	Snack Tray
#916	Pepper Shaker, 3¾"
#915	Salt Shaker, 3¾"
#918	Jug or Creamer, 8 Oz.

Row 2:

#925	Jug, 2 Pt.
#910	Bean Pot, 2 Qt.
#924	Individual Bean Pot, 12 Oz.

Row 3:

#923	Cookie Jar, 94 Oz.
#927	French Handled Casserole w/cover, 5¼"
#979	Covered French Handled Casserole, 3 Pt. w/Warmer (Rare)

Row 4:

#944	Oval Casserole & Cover, 2 Pt.
#914	Ice Jug, 2 Qt.
#963	Ash Tray w/Deer imprint, 8"

See brochure pages for additional molds available in this line. Note the reference "identified as the 900 series." This appears to be the only reference to identify this line.

Some of the dinnerware lines produced by Hull Pottery were not given specific names, however, it is easy to identify the Tangerine and Avocado lines by referencing their colors.

COUNTRY SQUIRE

The green agate from the Rainbow line was named Country Squire and another dinnerware line emerged. However, the mixing bowl molds used in this line were from Provincial, including #111 bake dish. The butter dish, pie plate, ice jug, and other items from this line that are not pictured in these brochures are listed in the index. Pieces from this line are, like the Tangerine pieces, difficult to find, however the collection can be supplemented with the Rainbow green agate pieces.

Row 1:

#100	Dinner Plate, 10¼"
#101	Salad Plate, 6½"
#103	Fruit Bowl, 5¼"
#102	Coffee Mug, 9 Oz.
#122	Coffee Pot, 60 Oz.

Row 2:

#105	Mixing Bowl, 5¼"
#106	Mixing Bowl, 6¾"
#107	Mixing Bowl, 8¼"
#109	Water Jug, 5 Pt.
#125	Jug, 2 Pt.
#118	Jug/Creamer, 8 Oz.

#149   Tea Pot

Row 3:

#110	Bean Pot, 2 Qt.
#124	Individual Bean Pot, 12 Oz.
#119	Sugar Bowl, 4"
#118	Creamer, 8 Oz.
#111	Bake Dish w/cover, 3 Pt.
#127	French Handled Casserole w/cover, 5¼"
#126	Beer Stein, 16 Oz.

Row 4:

#114	Ice Jug, 2 Qt.
#115	Salt Shaker, 3¾"
#116	Pepper Shaker, 3¾"
#121	Chip n' Dip Leaf, 15" x 10½"
#123	Cookie Jar, 94 Oz.

Country Squire SERVING-WARE

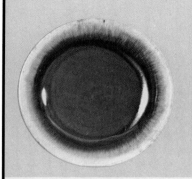

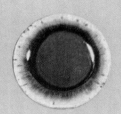

| 100 Dinner Plate 10¼" Dia. | 101 Salad Plate 6½" Dia. | 103 Fruit 5¼" | 102 Mug 9 oz. | 122 Coffee Pot w/cover (lock lid) 60 oz. |

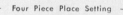
└─── Four Piece Place Setting ───┘

| 105 Mixing Bowl 5¼" | 106 Mixing Bowl 6¾" | 107 Mixing Bowl 8¼" | 109 Water Jug 5 pint | 125 Jug 2 pt. | 118 Jug ½ pt. |

| 110 Bean Pot w/cover 2 qt. | 124 Individual Bean Pot w/cover 12 oz. | 119 Sugar Bowl w/cover 4" Dia. | 118 Creamer 8 oz. | 111 Bake Dish 3 pt. 112 Casserole w/cover 3 pt. | 113 French Handled Casserole 5¼" 127 French Handled Casserole w/cover | 126 Beer Stein 16 oz. |

| 114 Ice Jug 2 qt. | 115 Salt Shaker w/cork 3¾" Hi. | 116 Pepper Shaker w/cork 3¾" Hi. | 121 Leaf Shaped Chip 'n Dip 15"X10½" | 123 Cookie Jar w/cover 94 oz. |

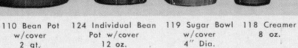

Row 1:

#141	Individual Oval Steak Plate, 11¾" x 9"
#142	Divided Vegetable
#143	Open Oval Baker

Row 2:

#144	Oval Casserole w/cover
#145	Salad or Spaghetti Bowl
#147	Plastic Fork and Spoon Set (not included in value guide)

Row 3:

#148	Oval Casserole w/cover
#149	Tea Pot w/cover, 5 Cup
#151	Jam or Mustard Jar, 12 Oz.

Row 4:

#153	Soup Mug, 11 Oz.
#154	Tray for Snack Set
#156	(Repeated)
#157	(Repeated)

Due to the limited production of this line, this set is difficult to complete. Most collectors purchase pieces from this line to compliment Rainbow collections; however, these pieces are still worth adding to your collection. This high-gloss dark green finish is very attractive, and mixes well with the Rainbow's brighter colors, tangerine and butterscotch.

Note: The coffee pot, salad plate, fruit bowl and salt and pepper set are displayed with the Rainbow line in the colored plate pictures.

#F69 Planter Imperial Duck Planter makes for a nice centerpiece to a Country Squire setting.

styled in *a beautiful blend of turquoise and green agate*

OVEN AND DETERGENT PROOF

141
Individual Oval Steak Plate
11¾" x 9"

142
Divided Vegetable
10¾" x 7¼"

143
Open Oval Baker
10" x 7¼"

146—Three piece Salad Set consisting of:
1 only #145—Salad Bowl
1 only #147—Fork & Spoon Set

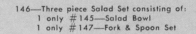

144
Oval Casserole & Cover
10" x 7¼" (3 pt.)

145
Salad or Spaghetti Bowl
10¼"

147—Fork and
Spoon Set

148
Oval Casserole & Cover
2 qt.—10" x 7¼"

149
Tea Pot & Cover
5 cup

151
Jam or Mustard Jar & Cover
Set with Spoon
12 oz.

#155—8 pc. Set
Consisting of:
4 only #153 Soup Mugs 11 oz.
4 only #154 Trays

#156—8 pc. Set
Consisting of:
4 only #102 Coffee Mugs 9 oz.
4 only #154 Trays

#157—8 pc. Set
Consisting of:
4 only #103 Cereal 12 oz.
4 only #154 Trays

Hull Pottery Company, Crooksville, Ohio

CRESTONE

A whole new set of molds was developed for this dinnerware line with the exception of the butter dish which was incorporated from the House 'n Garden line. Many feel that this line was Hull's attempt at producing dinnerware that would appeal to the Art Deco lovers. The bright turquoise color used for the Crestone glaze, as well as, the more simplistic style designed into the serving ware molds was popular during the Art Deco period.

The #331 luncheon plate, #330 saucer, #303 fruit bowl, #307 casserole w/cover, #314 custard cup and #305 carafe with companion stacking coffee cup #329 were immediately incorporated into the H&G line. Many of these pieces can be found in the H&G mirror brown glaze with the Crestone imprint as mentioned previously.

Row 1:

#303	Fruit Bowl, 6"
#302	Coffee Mug, 9 Oz.
#314	Custard Cup, 6 Oz.
#361	Butter Dish

Row 2:

#301	Salad or Dessert Plate
#319	Sugar Bowl, 8 Oz.
#318	Creamer, 8 Oz.
#304	Bread and Butter Plate, 6½"

Row 3:

#300	Dinner Plate, 10½"
#870C	Individual Oval Steak Plate, 11¾" x 9" (Note: Probably an Employee Special)
#331	Luncheon Plate, 9⅜"

Row 4:

#305	Carafe w/cover, 2 Cup (Difficult to Find)
#329	Cup, 7 Oz.
#330	Saucer, 5⅞" (Under #329)
#310	Gravy Boat, 10 Oz.
#311	Saucer for Gray Boat, 6½" (Under #310)
#326	Beverage Stein, 14 Oz.

Row 1:

#322	Coffee Server w/cover, 8 Cup
#325	Beverage Pitcher, 38 Oz.
#349	Tea Pot w/cover, 5 Cup

Row 2:

#871C	Well 'n Tree Steak Plate, 14" x 10" (Rare) (Note: Probably an Employee Special)
#315	Salt Shaker, 3¾"
#316	Pepper Shaker, 3¾"
#321	Chip 'n Dip Leaf, 14¼" x 10¼" (Hard to Find)

Row 3:

#345	Vegetable or Salad Bowl, 9¾"
#308	Individual Casserole w/cover, 9 Oz.
#307	Casserole w/cover, 32 Oz.

Not Shown:

| #313 | French Handled Casserole, 9 Oz. (See Brochure) |

This line is particularly favored by collectors due to its unusual and attractive color, as well as interesting mold designs. Country or contemporary, the Crestone line compliments a wide variety of decors. Note the embellished handles on the coffee server, beverage pitcher, beverage stein and tea pot. The #302 coffee mug handle is also different from the H&G coffee mug.

Note: Employee specials were frequent happenings at the Hull Pottery Company. Employees were permitted to work on personal items during off time and many created special items for their personal use, for gifts, or just for fun. These pieces, when located, are a great find and are highly prized by collectors.

for

casual living ---

325 Beverage Pitcher
38 oz.

326 Party
Beverage Stein
14 oz.

327 French Hdld.
Casserole w/Cover
9 oz.

329 Cup
7 oz.

330 Saucer
5 7/8 "

331 Luncheon Plate
9 3/8 "

345 Vegetable
or Salad Bowl
9 3/4 "
346 Salad Set
1—345 Salad Bowl
1—Wooden Fork
1—Wooden Spoon

349 Teapot
w/Cover
(5 Cup)

351 Mustard
or Jam Jar
w/Plastic Spoon

361 Butter Dish
w/Cover
1/4 lb. capacity

369 Onion Soup
or Salad Bowl
9 oz.

95—4 Pc. Coffee Carafé Set
1—305 Coffee Carafé
1—Cover
1—329 Coffee Cup 7 oz.
1—330 Deep Well Saucer

One outstanding feature also
in the design is that it permits
easy stacking that takes less
storage area.

Carafé holds 2 cups to start of neck
—no need to burn your fingers.
Ideal for casual living.

Notice the large platform
chimes on all items — far
superior to ordinary handles.

Gravy boat is separate
from saucer. No need to
ever spot the table cloth
now.

All casserole covers
have large deep rings
as knobs to serve as
glazed over Trivets
when inverted.

Look at the angle of
this. Our extra deep
wells in the saucers
will save many spills.

hull u.s.a.
Crestone ©
OVEN-PROOF

an
ovenproof
creation

hull pottery company —

300 Dinner Plate
10¼"

301 Salad
or Dessert Plate
7½"

302 Coffee Mug
9 oz.

303 Fruit
6"

304 Bread
and Butter Plate
6½"

305 Carafé
w/Cover
(2 Cup)

306 Open Baker
32 oz.

307 Casserole
w/Cover
32 oz.

308 Indiv. Casserole
w/Cover
9 oz.

310 Gravy Boat
or Syrup
10 oz.

311 Saucer For
Gravy Boat or Syrup
6½"
312 Two Piece Gravy Boat Set

313 French Handled
Casserole
9 oz.

crooksville, ohio *u.s.a.*

314 Custard Cup
6 oz.

315 Salt Shaker
3¾"
316 Pepper Shaker
3¾"
317 Salt and Pepper Set

318 Creamer
8 oz.

319 Sugar Bowl
w/Cover
8 oz.
320 Sugar and Creamer Set

321 Chip 'n Dip Leaf
14¼"x10¼"x2¼"

322 Coffee Server
w/Cover
(8 Cup)

AVOCADO

Remember when everything from the kitchen appliances to the carpet on the floor was avocado! This dinnerware line can easily be dated by its colored glaze to the 1960's when the avocado color was popular. Like the Tangerine and Country Squire lines, this dinnerware line consists of relatively few decorative molds; however, special pieces can be found such as the #635A Roaster and #687A and #688A Mushroom Salt & Pepper set! The glaze is similar to the one used in the Heritageware line of the 1950's, which consisted of kitchenware molds. The Heritageware line was not a complete dinnerware line, however, it is often confused with the Avocado line.

Also note that this line was also produced using the Crestone molds and sold as a starter set under #670. These Crestone mold pieces are relatively difficult to find however, and may or may not be marked Crestone. Avocado is one of the easier colored glaze lines to collect as it was produced for three years and more quantities are available for collectors.

Row 1:

#642	Divided Vegetable Dish, 10¾" x 7¼"
#697	Coffee Cup, 7 Oz.
#698	Saucer (under #697)
#602	Mug, 9 Oz.
#641	Oval Steak Plate, 11¾" x 9"

Row 2:

#699	Luncheon Plate, 9⅜"
#600	Dinner Plate, 10¼"
#601	Salad Plate, 6½"
#669	Soup/Salad Bowl, 6½"

Row 3:

#633	Fruit Bowl, 6"
#626	Beer Stein, 16 Oz.
#666	Pie Plate, 9¼"
#627	French Handled Casserole w/cover, 12 Oz.
#674	Oval Bake 'n Serve Dish, 10" x 5"

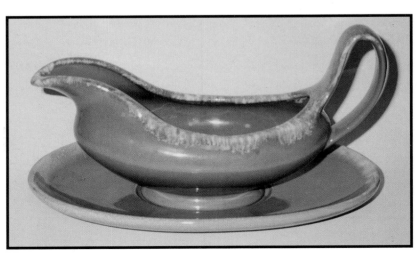

#689A Gravy Boat w/Tray
(Rare Find)

#690A   Chip 'n Dip (2) pieces 12" x 11" six-sided. Also a rare find, this set is extremely difficult to find in the House 'n Garden mirror brown. So this Avocado issue is an especially prized item by Avocado collectors!

All of the molds used in the Avocado line are from the original House 'n Garden line. To date no other unusual and unique molds have been identified for this line, but so many items were made outside of production by employees that there will be many new items turn up in the future.

Row 1:

#635A	Rectangular Roaster w/cover, 7 Pt., (Rare)
#616	Pepper Shaker, 3¾"
#615	Salt Shaker, 3¾"
#621	Chip 'n Dip Leaf

Row 2:

#622	Coffee Pot w/cover, 8 Cup
#624	Individual Bean Pot w/cover, 12 Oz. Note: The only difference between #651 and #624 is the slotted lid.
#610	Bean Pot w/cover, 2 Qt
#651	Jam or Mustard Jar, 12 Oz.
#648	Deep Oval Casserole w/cover, 2 Qt.

Row 3:

#688A	Mushroom Pepper Shaker, 3¾"
#687A	Mushroom Salt Shaker, 3¾"
#661	Covered Butter Dish
#618	Creamer, 8 Oz.
#649	Tea Pot w/cover, 5 Cup
#625	Jug, 2 Pt.

for the new way of life . . .

OVENPROOF House 'n Garden Serving-ware

FOR YOUR DAILY NEEDS

669
6½" Soup/Salad

600 Dinner Plate
10¼" Dia.

602 Mug
9 oz.

603 Fruit
5¼"

601 Salad Plate
6½"

604—4 PIECE PLACE SETTING

615 Salt Shaker
w/cork 3¾" Hi.

616 Pepper Shaker
w/cork 3¾" Hi.

618
Creamer 8 oz.

619 Sugar Bowl
w/Cover 12 oz.

627 Fr. Handled Casserole
w/Cover 12 oz.

633 Fruit
6"

626 Beer Stein
16 oz.

617 Salt & Pepper Set   620 Sugar & Creamer Set

622 Coffee Pot
w/Cover 8 Cup

649 Tea Pot
w/Cover 5 Cup

625 Jug
2 pt.

621 Chip 'n Dip

641 Oval Steak Plate
11¾" x 9"

642 Divided Vegetable Dish
10¾" x 7¼"

648 Deep Oval Casserole
w/Cover 2 qt.

hull pottery company — crooksville, ohio u.s.a

70

AVOCADO *with Ivory trim*

666 Pie Plate	624 Ind. Bean Pot	610 Bean Pot	699 Luncheon Plate
9 ¼ " Dia.	w/Cover 12 oz.	w/Cover 2 qt.	9 ⅜ " Dia.

698 Saucer	697 Cup	651 Jam or Mustard Jar w/Cover Set w/Spoon 12 oz.	661 Covered Butter Dish (¼ lb. Capacity)	674 Oval Bake 'n Serve Dish
5 ⅞ "	7 oz.			10" x 5" x 1 ⅜ "

624-4 Beer Stein 16 oz.
4 Piece Party Pack Set
(Individual Carton 6 Sets to Master)

604—Oven Proof 16 Piece Starter Set   **670—Oven Proof 16 Piece Starter Set**

4 - Fruits—5 ¼ "	4 - Salad Plates—6 ½ "
4 - Mugs—9 oz.	4 - Dinner Plates—10 ¼ " Dia.

4 - Fruits—6"	4 - Saucers—5 ⅞ "
4 - Cups—7 oz.	4 - Luncheon Plates—9 ⅜ " Dia.

MIRROR ALMOND

This dinnerware line was marketed as Mirror Almond with Caramel Trim. Many Crooksville residents remember this line as one that was sold from the back of a truck at the annual pottery festival. This ivory/almond glaze was contrasted with a brown/caramel trim. Some items have a darker contrast trim, almost mirror brown, while some can be found entirely devoid of trim.

This relatively rare line was produced in the basic starter set, with several accessory pieces. Those items not shown in these pictures are listed in the index. Among the items produced in this line were the divided vegetable dish, french handled casserole, snack set, 16 Oz. mug, mixing bowls, oval serving dish, ramekins and gingerbread platter and an unusual vinegar cruet.

Picture 1:

   Top Row:

#800	Dinner Plate, 10¼"
#887	Mushroom Salt Shaker
#804	Luncheon Plate, 8½"
#888	Mushroom Pepper Shaker
#801	Salad Plate, 6½"

   Bottom Row:

#869	Soup or Salad Bowl, 6½"
#867	Handled Vegetable Bowl, 11" x 8¾"
#802	Mug, 9 Oz.
#803	Fruit Bowl, 5¼"

Picture 2:

#818	Creamer, 10 Oz.
#805	Cup, 6 Oz.
#819	Sugar Bowl w/lid, 12 Oz.

Picture 3: (Note the dark trim on these items.)

#867	Handled Vegetable Bowl, 11" x 8¾"
#887	Mushroom Salt Shaker
#888	Mushroom Pepper Shaker (Note the difference in glaze finishes.)
#841	Individual Oval Steak Plate

Picture 1: (Courtesy of Lori Friend of Statesville, North Carolina.)

Picture 2: Note the light colored trim as compared to the pieces displaced in Picture 3.

Picture 3: The trim on these items is very dark.

for the new way of life . . .

OVENPROOF **House 'n Garden** *Serving-ware*

FOR YOUR DAILY USE

THE UNITED STATES · GLAZE TESTED APPROVED · POTTERS ASSOCIATION

836 — 6" Mixing Bowl

837 — 7" Mixing Bowl

838 — 8" Mixing Bowl

839 — 3 Pc. Mixing Bowl Set (1 each #836-837-838)

MIRROR ALMOND WITH CARAMEL TRIM

869 — 6½" Soup or Salad Bowl

853 — 11 Oz. Soup Mug

854 — 9½" × 6¼" Tray

855 — 8 Pc. Soup 'n Sandwich Set (4 each #853-854)

hull pottery company

- crooksville, ohio 43731 *u.s.a.*

6/81/2M

THE RIDGE LINES

The early 80's brought a whole new line of mold designs to the Hull Pottery kilns. The Ridge lines were marketed as new, highly functional, casual serving ware. The name was derived from the distinctive ridge design and also for the various local geographical ridges found in the Crooksville, Ohio area. The design of these new dinnerware lines reflected the effort by management to update their marketable products. Competition was fierce, sales were low and no new national accounts had been established for many years. These contemporary styled molds were produced in Flint (Gray), Tawny (Sand) and Walnut (Brown).

While the lines were limited to only 13 molds, many accessory pieces were issued in the three colors. These accessories are included in this section, but are listed in the index under Accessories by color (Gray or Sand). However, the mirror brown accessory pieces are listed in the index under House 'n Garden/Mirror Brown.

The accessories produced in the sand and gray are more difficult to find than those with the mirror brown glaze. It is believed that the mirror brown was produced in larger quantities and over a longer period than the sand and gray glazes.

#600   Ramekins. The actual uses for this small dish are in question, but many believe it was produced as a jelly server. Conversely, Larry Taylor indicated that the piece was produced from waste parts!

#1566 Pie Plate
#1600 Ramekins
#1561 Butter Dish
These gray Accessory pieces
are difficult to find.

Row 1:

#102	Mug, 10 Oz. (Accessory)
#1549	Tea Pot (Accessory)
#104	Cup, 8 Oz. (Ridge)
#105	Saucer, 6" (Ridge)

Row 2:

#1571	Continental Mug, 12 Oz. (Accessory)
#176	Custard Cup, 8 Oz. (Accessory)
#103	Bowl, 5½" (Ridge)
#108	Vegetable Bowl, 7½" (Ridge)
#1526	Stein, 18 Oz. (Accessory)

Row 3:

#100	Dinner Plate, 10¼" (Ridge)
#101	Salad Plate, 7¼" (Ridge)
#115	Steak Plate , 9½" x 12" (Ridge)

Note: Many of the House 'n Garden items that were continued as accessory pieces in the 80's were in some cases larger than the original molds of earlier years; as indicated by the volumes listed in the brochures following. However, I have found that this sizing is not significantly noticeable for the three glazes issued later and the original molds. Because the differences are so minor and these items also have the same factory assigned number as the earlier productions, these larger items are not listed separately in the value guide.

One exception to the mold enlargements that resulted in a new production number, however, is the issue of the #302 mug which is listed as 10 Oz. vs the #502 mug from the H&G line which was listed as 9 Oz. Note the square cut in the handle of #302. While the original starter set from H&G line (#504) continued to be offered, the #502 mug mold was replaced with the #302 mold in the set.

Row 1:

#1518	Creamer, 10 Oz.* (Accessory)
#110	Creamer, 8 Oz. (Ridge)
#113	Pepper, 3" (Ridge)
#111	Salt, 3" (Ridge)
#109	Sugar, 8 Oz. (Ridge)
#1524	Individual Bean Pot (Accessory)

Row 2:

#160	4-Piece Canister Set (Accessory)

Row 3:

#1595	Handled Skillet, 18 Oz. (Accessory)
#15280	Casserole w/Duck cover (Accessory)

Row 4:

#1196	Sitting Pig Bank (Accessory)
#1568	Square Banker (Accessory)
#1195	Corky Pig Bank (Accessory)

#1507 32 Oz. Casserole
(Note: The mold is from the
Crestone line.)

* While this piece is listed in the brochures following as a 10 Oz. container, I have compared it to the older, H&G version and find them to be identical in size, shape and volume.

All the Ridge items are difficult to find, and the Flint/Gray and Tawny/Sand items are particularly difficult to find in the accessory pieces.

Also, included with the following brochures for the Ridge lines is a price list from January of 1982 which references all the factory assigned numbers for the three glazes.

This plate picture contains a mixture of Ridge, the accessories and a few pieces from the Ring line covered in the next section. Because of the limited number of pieces and colors from the various lines, it was necessary to combine them into one plate picture.

The first row contains five pieces from the Ring line which will be covered in more depth in the next few pages.

Row 1:

#5436	Mixing Bowl, 6" (Ring)	
$5438	Mixing Bowl, 8" (Ring)	
#5449	Coffee Pot, 5 Cup (Ring)	
#5418	Creamer (Ring)	
#5402	Coffee Cup (Ring)	

Row 2:

#573	Small Oval Serving Dish, 9½ Oz. (Accessory)
#310	Creamer, 8 Oz. (Walnut/Ridge)
#313	Pepper Shaker, 3" (Walnut/Ridge)
#303	Bowl, 8 Oz. (Walnut/Ridge)
#302	Mug, 10 Oz. (Walnut/Ridge & Accessory)
#301	Salad Plate, 7¼" (Walnut/Ridge)

Row 3:

#360	Canister Set (Stacking) (Accessory)
#315	Steak Plate, 9½" x 12" (Walnut/Ridge)
#535	Onion Soup w/cover (Accessory)

Row 4:

#2595	Handled Skillet, 18 Oz. (Accessory)
#2525	Jug, 36 Oz. (Accessory)
#2526	Stein, 18 Oz. (Accessory)
#202	Mug, 10 Oz. (Tawny/Ridge & Accessory)
#204	Cup, 8 Oz. (Tawny/Ridge)
#205	Saucer, 6" (Tawny/Ridge)

It's not difficult to understand why House 'n Garden collectors would want to add these Walnut/Ridge and brown accessories to their collections. The glaze is identical to the original mirror brown from the House 'n Garden line, including the foam drip decoration in most cases.

Note: The 10 Oz. Mug makes its appearance in both the Ridge lines and as an accessory. This crossing-over from one line to another can be confusing for beginning collectors. During the 80's, many changes were taking place at the Hull Pottery; not only in the molds being produced, but also in the marketing of the various new lines. Hopefully, pointing out these duplications, along with the printing of the full line of brochures included in this publication will eliminate some of the confusion.

Flint Ridge

12 pc. Set
4 ea. Dinner Plate, Bowl, Mug

16 pc. Set
4 ea. Dinner Plate, Salad Plate, Bowl, Mug

20 pc. Set
4 ea. Dinner Plate, Salad Plate, Bowl, Cup, Saucer

Completer Set
1 ea. Sugar w/Cover, Creamer, Vegetable Bowl, Steak Plate

6 pc. Snack Set
2 ea. Tray, Bowl, Mug

Sugar & Creamer Set

Salt & Pepper Set

Tawny Ridge

12 pc. Set
4 ea. Dinner Plate, Bowl, Mug

16 pc. Set
4 ea. Dinner Plate, Salad Plate, Bowl, Mug

20 pc. Set
4 ea. Dinner Plate, Salad Plate, Bowl, Cup, Saucer

Completer Set
1 ea. Sugar w/Cover, Creamer, Vegetable Bowl, Steak Plate

6 pc. Snack Set
2 ea. Tray, Bowl, Mug

Sugar & Creamer Set

Salt & Pepper Set

Walnut Ridge

12 pc. Set
4 ea. Dinner Plate, Bowl, Mug

16 pc. Set
4 ea. Dinner Plate, Salad Plate, Bowl, Mug

20 pc. Set
4 ea. Dinner Plate, Salad Plate, Bowl, Cup, Saucer

Completer Set
1 ea. Sugar w/Cover, Creamer, Vegetable Bowl, Steak Plate

6 pc. Snack Set
2 ea. Tray, Bowl, Mug

Sugar & Creamer Set

Salt & Pepper Set

See price list for open stock.

PRICE LIST

HULL POTTERY
CROOKSVILLE, OHIO
SINCE 1903
327 AMERINE STREET
CROOKSVILLE, OHIO 43731
614/982-2075

"TERMS OF SALE"

Sold only in standard packages — no extra packing charge
Terms: Net 30 days — fob Crooksville, Ohio —
1½% Per Month Charge will be added after 30 days.
Positively no allowance for breakage — claims must be filed with common carrier.
No goods returned without our permission.
Warranty is neither expressed nor implied.

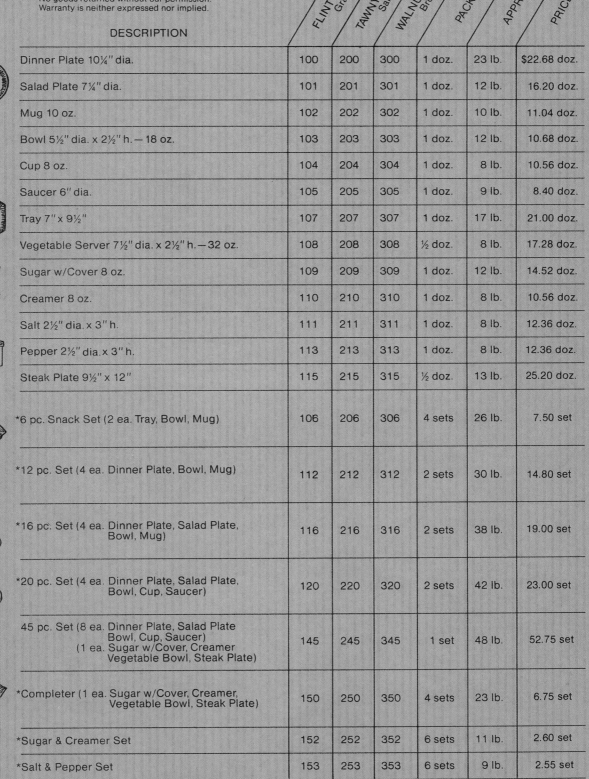

DESCRIPTION	FLINT RIDGE Gray	TAWNY RIDGE Sand	WALNUT RIDGE Brown	PACKED	APPROX. WT.	PRICE
Dinner Plate 10¼" dia.	100	200	300	1 doz.	23 lb.	$22.68 doz.
Salad Plate 7¼" dia.	101	201	301	1 doz.	12 lb.	16.20 doz.
Mug 10 oz.	102	202	302	1 doz.	10 lb.	11.04 doz.
Bowl 5½" dia. x 2½" h. — 18 oz.	103	203	303	1 doz.	12 lb.	10.68 doz.
Cup 8 oz.	104	204	304	1 doz.	8 lb.	10.56 doz.
Saucer 6" dia.	105	205	305	1 doz.	9 lb.	8.40 doz.
Tray 7" x 9½"	107	207	307	1 doz.	17 lb.	21.00 doz.
Vegetable Server 7½" dia. x 2½" h. — 32 oz.	108	208	308	½ doz.	8 lb.	17.28 doz.
Sugar w/Cover 8 oz.	109	209	309	1 doz.	12 lb.	14.52 doz.
Creamer 8 oz.	110	210	310	1 doz.	8 lb.	10.56 doz.
Salt 2½" dia. x 3" h.	111	211	311	1 doz.	8 lb.	12.36 doz.
Pepper 2½" dia. x 3" h.	113	213	313	1 doz.	8 lb.	12.36 doz.
Steak Plate 9½" x 12"	115	215	315	½ doz.	13 lb.	25.20 doz.
*6 pc. Snack Set (2 ea. Tray, Bowl, Mug)	106	206	306	4 sets	26 lb.	7.50 set
*12 pc. Set (4 ea. Dinner Plate, Bowl, Mug)	112	212	312	2 sets	30 lb.	14.80 set
*16 pc. Set (4 ea. Dinner Plate, Salad Plate, Bowl, Mug)	116	216	316	2 sets	38 lb.	19.00 set
*20 pc. Set (4 ea. Dinner Plate, Salad Plate, Bowl, Cup, Saucer)	120	220	320	2 sets	42 lb.	23.00 set
45 pc. Set (8 ea. Dinner Plate, Salad Plate Bowl, Cup, Saucer) (1 ea. Sugar w/Cover, Creamer Vegetable Bowl, Steak Plate)	145	245	345	1 set	48 lb.	52.75 set
*Completer (1 ea. Sugar w/Cover, Creamer, Vegetable Bowl, Steak Plate)	150	250	350	4 sets	23 lb.	6.75 set
*Sugar & Creamer Set	152	252	352	6 sets	11 lb.	2.60 set
*Salt & Pepper Set	153	253	353	6 sets	9 lb.	2.55 set

*Full Color Label — Individual Carton (All Capacities To Brim)

2/82/5C

ACCESSORIES

The following brochures contain all of the accessory pieces that were offered during the production of the Ridge and subsequent lines. Most of the brown pieces in these brochures are identical to those listed under the House 'n Garden lines, including having the same factory assigned number. A few new molds are introduced here, however, such as the #360 (4) piece stacking canister set, the #314 (32) Oz. covered casserole, the #535 Onion Soup, and the #3505 garlic cellar, etc.

Also, many of these repeat molds are advertised in larger volumes than the original productions, however, the differences are only slight and the factory assigned number is the same.

In a few instances, a new size resulted in a new factory assigned number, such as the #527 (12) Oz. French Handled Casserole and the #573 Small Oval Serving Dish.

Due to the crossing over of many of the brown pieces in these brochures from the House 'n Garden line, all brown items are listed with the House 'n Garden line in the value guide, while the sand and gray are listed separately under Accessories.

The Gingerbread pieces represented in another section are also listed in these brochures, however, the child's cup and bowl had not yet been produced at the printing of this brochure.

You will find that the Gingerbread pieces are also displayed in the Ring line, which included the child's cup and bowl. These pieces are listed in the index under Gingerbread.

64 OZ. COFFEE SERVER W/COVER
1522 GRAY
2522 SAND
522 BROWN

80 OZ. WATER JUG
1509 GRAY
2509 SAND
509 BROWN

72 OZ. ICE JUG
1514 GRAY
2514 SAND
514 BROWN

32 OZ. CASSEROLE W/COVER
1507 GRAY
2507 SAND
507 BROWN

80 OZ. BEAN POT W/COVER
1510 GRAY
2510 SAND
510 BROWN

10 OZ. MUG
102 GRAY
202 SAND
302 BROWN

12 OZ. FRUIT
503 BROWN

10 OZ. CREAMER
1518 GRAY
2518 SAND
518 BROWN

SALAD PLATE, 6½"
501 BROWN

DINNER PLATE 10¼"
500 BROWN

STARTER SET
504 BROWN
4-10¼" DINNER PLATES
4-6½" SALAD PLATES
4-10 OZ. MUGS
4-12 OZ. FRUITS

87

96 OZ. COOKIE
JAR W/COVER
1523 GRAY
2523 SAND
523 BROWN

36 OZ. JUG
1525 GRAY
2525 SAND
525 BROWN

3 PC. MIXING
BOWL SET, (6"-7"-
8")
1539 GRAY
2539 SAND
539 BROWN

60 OZ. MIXING BOWL
W/POURING SPOUT, 8"
1538 GRAY
2538 SAND
538 BROWN

21 OZ. MIXING
BOWL, 6"
1536 GRAY
2536 SAND
536 BROWN

40 OZ. MIXING
BOWL, 7"
1537 GRAY
2537 SAND
537 BROWN

18 OZ. STEIN
1526 GRAY
2526 SAND
526 BROWN

12 OZ. ONION
SOUP W/COVER
1535 GRAY
2535 SAND
535 BROWN

12 OZ. ONION SOUP
1534 GRAY
2534 SAND
534 BROWN

INDIVIDUAL
OVAL STEAK
PLATE
541 BROWN

13 OZ.
INDIVIDUAL
BEAN POT
W/COVER
1524 GRAY
2524 SAND
524 BROWN

12 OZ. FRENCH
HANDLED
CASSEROLE
1513 GRAY
2513 SAND
513 BROWN

12 OZ. FRENCH
HANDLED
CASSEROLE
W/COVER
1527 GRAY
2527 SAND
527 BROWN

88

**4 PC. CANISTER
SET**
160 GRAY
260 SAND
360 BROWN

**GINGERBREAD
MAN COOKIE
JAR**
123 GRAY
223 SAND
323 BROWN

**38 OZ.
CASSEROLE
W/DUCK COVER**
15280 GRAY
25280 SAND
5280 BROWN

**68 OZ. CASSEROLE
W/CHICKEN
COVER**
15850 GRAY
25850 SAND
5850 BROWN

**SITTING
PIGGY
BANK**
1196 GRAY
2196 SAND
196 BROWN

**32 OZ.
CASSEROLE
W/COVER**
114 GRAY
214 SAND
314 BROWN

CORKY PIGGY BANK
1195 GRAY
2195 SAND
195 BROWN

**18 OZ. SERVER
W/HANDLE**
1595 GRAY
2595 SAND
595 BROWN

**13 OZ. GARLIC
CELLAR**
1505 GRAY
2505 SAND
3505 BROWN

**GINGERBREAD
BOY COASTER/
SPOON REST,
5" x 5"**
199 GRAY
299 SAND
399 BROWN

**GINGERBREAD
MAN SERVER, 10" x 10"**
1198 GRAY
2198 SAND
198 BROWN

89

12 OZ. CONTINENTAL MUG
1571 GRAY
2571 SAND
571 BROWN

21 OZ. SOUP OR SALAD BOWL
1569 GRAY
2569 SAND
569 BROWN

50 OZ. SQUARE BAKER
1568 GRAY
2568 SAND
568 BROWN

PIE PLATE, 9¼"
1566 GRAY
2566 SAND
566 BROWN

34 OZ. INDIVIDUAL OVAL SPAGHETTI PLATE
1581 GRAY
2581 SAND
581 BROWN

OVAL WELL 'N TREE STEAK PLATE
593 BROWN

9 OZ. FRENCH HANDLED CASSEROLE W/COVER
579 BROWN

9 OZ. FRENCH HANDLED CASSEROLE
562 BROWN

16 OZ. OVAL SERVING DISH
1574 GRAY
2574 SAND
574 BROWN

9½ OZ. SMALL OVAL SERVING DISH
1573 GRAY
2573 SAND
573 BROWN

BAKE & SERVE, 6½"
1589 GRAY
2589 SAND
589 BROWN

8 OZ. CUSTARD CUP
176 GRAY
276 SAND
376 BROWN

MUSHROOM SALT & PEPPER SET
587/588 BROWN

2½ OZ. RAMEKIN
1600 GRAY
2600 SAND
600 BROWN

68 OZ. DEEP
OVAL
CASSEROLE
W/COVER
1548 GRAY
2548 SAND
 548 BROWN

90 OZ. SALAD
OR SPAGHETTI
BOWL, 10¼"
1545 GRAY
2545 SAND
 545 BROWN

38 OZ. OVAL
CASSEROLE
W/COVER
1544 GRAY
2644 SAND
 544 BROWN

40 OZ. TEA POT
AND COVER
1549 GRAY
2549 SAND
 549 BROWN

TRAY, 9½" x 5¾"
1554 GRAY
2554 SAND
 554 BROWN

14 OZ. SOUP MUG
1553 GRAY
2553 SAND
 553 BROWN

BUTTER DISH
W/COVER
1561 GRAY
2561 SAND
 561 BROWN

13 OZ. JAM OR
MUSTARD JAR
W/COVER
1550 GRAY
2550 SAND
 550 BROWN

THE NEW BROWN RING

According to Larry Taylor, president of Hull Pottery, this line was never officially named. As a collector, I have referred to this line by the rings in the design on the outside of the molds for several years. Thus for purposes of identification, I will refer to this dinnerware line as Ring in this publication.

During the final years, a whole new line of molds were designed to compete with the Pfaltzgraff dinnerware that had won the J.C. Penney account from Hull. As the story goes per Mr. Taylor, a J.C. Penney's buyer with whom the Hull Pottery was attempting to negotiate a new national account told the Hull Pottery salesman that J.C. Penney might be interested if Hull's lines were more competitive with Pfaltzgraff. Thus these new designs were created which resembled the Pfaltzgraff lines, in an effort to regain the J.C. Penney business. In fact, Hull retained Maury Mountain, a free-lance designer who was responsible for much of Pfaltzgraff's dinnerware designs to create these molds!

These new molds were produced in the brown, white and ivory. The white and ivory lines were named Country Belle and Heartland, and were finished with a painted decoration similar to the Pfaltzgraff designs. (These lines are included in the following sections.)

Row 1:

#5400	Dinner Plate
#5401	Salad Plate
#5402	Coffee Cup
#5403	Soup Bowl, 12 Oz.
#5442	Soup Bowl, 20 Oz. (Not Shown)
#5405	Saucer

Row 2:

#5473	Bowl for Bowl & Pitcher
#5470	Pitcher, 36 Oz. (Not Shown)
#5472	Pitcher, 66 Oz.
#5441	Platter/Steak Plate
#5408	Vegetable/Serving Bowl
#5419	Sugar Bowl w/cover
#5418	Creamer

Row 3:

#195	Corky Pig (House 'n Garden)
#196	Sitting Pig (House 'n Garden)
#5462	Cheese Server (Unlabeled)
#5453	Salt & Pepper Set (Unlabeled)
#5449	Coffee Pot
#5850	Casserole w/Chicken cover (House 'n Garden)
#5280	Casserole w/Duck cover (House 'n Garden)
#5471	Stemmed Coffee Cup
#5476	Custard Cup
#5428	Casserole w/cover
#5422	Gravy Boat & Saucer (Set)

5414 5 Piece Place Setting
Consists of 1 each:
5400, 5401, 5402, 5403, 5404

5435 Completer Set
Consists of 1 each:
5408, 5441, 5452

5404 16 Piece Set
Consists of 4 each:
5400, 5401, 5402, 5403

504 Starter Set
Consists of 4 each:
500, 501, 503, 302

504 Starter Set
Consists of 4 each:
500 Dinner Plate 10¼"
501 Salad Plae 6½"
502 Fruit 5¼"
302 Mug 10 oz.

5414 5 Pc. Place Setting consists of 1 each: 5400, 5401, 5402, 5403, 5404

5470 - 36 oz. Pitcher   **5472** - 66 oz. Pitcher

5435 Completer Set consists of 1 each: 5408, 5441, 5452

198

325

399

323

324

5490

5423

5410

539
3 Pc.
Mixing Bowl
Set (6-7-8")

5439
3 Pc.
Mixing Bowl
Set (6-8-10")

567

5466

568

566

595

517

508

5439 — Consists of 1 each: **5436, 5438, 5440**

Note the House 'n Garden pieces included in this brochure, as well as the Gingerbread set which had been expanded by this time to include the child's cup and bowl.

The pieces in this brochure that are from the House 'n Garden line and the Gingerbread line are listed under House 'n Garden and Gingerbread in the index and are not included as part of the Ring listing.

Row 1:

See:	Gingerbread

Row 2:

#5490	Canister Set 4 Pieces
#5423	Cookie Jar *
#5410	Bean Pot *

Row 3:

#539	Mixing Bowl Set, 6" 7" & 8" (House 'n Garden)
#5436	Mixing Bowl, 6"
#5438	Mixing Bowl, 8"
#5440	Mixing Bowl, 10"
#567	Rectangular Baker

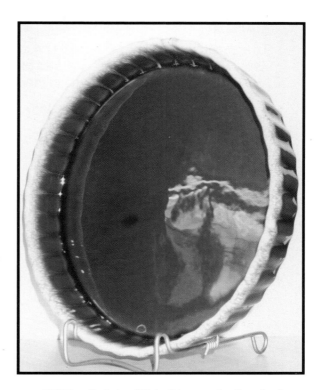

#508   Quiche Dish (House 'n Garden)

#568	Square Baker (House 'n Garden)
#595	Handled Skillet (House 'n Garden)
#517	Souffle Dish
#5466	Large Round Casserole
#566	Pie Plate (House 'n Garden)
#508	Quiche Dish

* These pieces are a separate offering from the 4-piece canister set, although the molds are the same. None of the pieces, neither the canisters, the cookie jar nor the bean pot are labeled or imprinted.

The beautiful design that is so attractive to collectors, coupled with the fact this line was only produced for a relatively short time, makes these pieces more expensive and difficult to find. House 'n Garden collectors are delighted to find pieces from this series to compliment their collections!

HEARTLAND

This ivory glazed dinnerware line was trimmed with a buttercup yellow drip and finished with a stenciled heart pattern in soft brown. The molds are identical to the Country Belle and Ring, and bear a striking resemblance to Pfaltzgraff dinnerware.

These pictures are from the collection belonging to Royce and Stella Frash of Crooksville, Ohio. Royce and Stella are collectors of the Heartland line as well as Hull Pottery dealers and have quite a few great items in their collection.

Picture 1:

#471	Stemmed Coffee Cup
#401	Salad Plate
#403	Soup Bowl, 12 Oz.
#400	Dinner Plate
#402	Coffee Cup
#405	Saucer

Picture 2:

#408	Vegetable/Serving Bowl
#441	Platter/Steak Plate
#419	Sugar Bowl w/cover
#418	Creamer

Picture 3:

#472	Pitcher, 66 Oz.
#470	Pitcher, 36 Oz.
#418	Creamer

Notice the differences in the yellow trim on these pieces. Some pieces can be found entirely devoid of any trim, and are probably seconds. These pieces are extremely difficult to find due to the limited production of this line.

PICTURE 1

PICTURE 3

PICTURE 2

For collectors, these pieces are difficult to spot. The pattern and markings are so similar to Pfaltzgraff pieces, that a close examination is needed for beginners to verify the Hull markings.

Picture 4:

#463	Cheese Server
#453	Salt Shaker, (Part of Set)
#449	Coffee Pot
#422	Gravy Boat & Saucer
#453	Pepper Shaker, (Part of Set)

Picture 5:

#474	Bowl and Pitcher Set (66 Pitcher)

Picture 6:

#467	Rectangular Baker
#444	Quiche Dish
#476	Custard Cup
#N/A	Test Piece (Unknown Mold w/Heartland Design)

See the brochure pages following for other items in this line. Note the casseroles with the duck and chicken covers carried over from the House 'n Garden lines! There is also an unnamed and unmarked condiment server #462.

The brown heart trim pieces in this pattern compliment those in the Ring line, and many collectors mix & match these sets.

PICTURE 4

PICTURE 6

PICTURE 5

472   470   418

HULL POTTERY
CROOKSVILLE, OHIO
SINCE 1903

327 AMERINE STREET
CROOKSVILLE, OHIO 43731
614/982-2075   614/982-2085

490

410   COOKIES   BAKED BEANS   423

439 3 pc. Bowl Set

436 6" Bowl   438 8" Bowl   440 10" Bowl

467   466   417   468   495   444

404 16 Piece Place Setting
Consists of 4 each:
400, 401, 402, 403

406 4 Piece Place Setting
Consists of 1 each:
400, 401, 402, 403

414 5 Piece Place Setting
Consists of 1 each:
400, 401, 402, 403, 405

420 20 Piece Place Setting
Consists of 4 each:
400, 401, 402, 403, 405

414 5 Piece Place Setting

474 Pitcher & Bowl Set

435 Completer Set

452 Sugar & Creamer Set

435 Completer Set   Consists of 1 each: 408, 441, 452

453 Set

101

COUNTRY BELLE
"BlueBelle"

This is another variation of the molds that were used in the Ring and Heartland lines. The pottery was glazed an off-white and finished with a stenciled blue flower and bell design. The country motif of this design is very popular and these pieces are not easily found.

This line has also been referred to as BlueBelle.

The pieces in these pictures on the following pages are from the private collection of Larry Taylor, president of Hull Pottery, of Crooksville, Ohio.

Picture 1:

#6471	Stemmed Coffee Cup
#6402	Coffee Cup
#6449	Coffee Pot
#6419	Sugar Bowl w/cover
#6418	Creamer

Picture 2:

#6568	Square Baker
#6440	Large Mixing Bowl
#6436	Small Mixing Bowl

Picture 3:

#6400	Dinner Plate
#6453	Salt & Pepper Set
#6423	Cookie Jar
#6422	Gravy Boat
#6403	Soup/Salad Bowl

The dinnerware reflects the country motif for which the line was designed. Also note #6466 is a large round casserole dish. The molds from this issue are identical to those in the Heartland line.

PICTURE 1: *Coffee Service*

PICTURE 2: *Serving Dishes*

PICTURE 3: *Table Service & Cookie Jar*

Note: All dinnerware pieces are listed in the value guide and pieces can be identified by referring to Heartland brochures. The last three digits of the CountryBelle numbers are the same as the Heartland numbers.

GINGERBREAD

The Gingerbread series is currently one of the most popular collectibles of the Hull Pottery lines; appealing to collectors in many different arenas. Collectors of cookie jars and train memorabilia, particularly, compete with Hull collectors to acquire these much coveted pieces.

The Gingerbread series, with the exception of the child's cup and bowl, was manufactured in mirror brown, gray and sand. Prior to the closing of the Crooksville plant, many of the cookie jars were subcontracted to the Western Stoneware pottery in Illinois due to the factory strike. One method for identifying the manufacture site of these jars is to examine the unglazed bottom edges of the head and base. These unglazed edges on the Ohio pieces are a chalky white; while the Illinois pieces are a grayish color due to the difference in the clay used for the molds. Some collectors place a higher value on the pieces manufactured at the Crooksville plant, despite the fact that the molds and glazes are identical. However, most collectors are happy simply to have acquired a piece for their collections, regardless of the origin of manufacture.

The Gingerbread Train canister set is by far the most sought after collectible of this series. Factory records indicate only approximately 16 sets were produced during the testing phase, however, collectors claim over 30 complete sets exist. None of these pieces were marked with the Hull imprint. (Production was never completed due to the closing of the factory, and no mark had yet been included in the molds during testing.)

As of this writing, stories of backroom reproductions are circulating, and a buyer must be absolutely confident of the seller before purchasing these pieces.

#802G Gingerbread Train Canister Set

| #802G1 | #802G2 | #802G3 | #802G4 |
| Engine | Coal Car | Passenger Car | Caboose |

This photo depicts a Japanese reproduction of the Gingerbread Boy Coaster/Spoon Rest. Note: The reproductions are on the right and left, the original is in the center. The reproduction is correct in details, however it is about ½" smaller, darker with a grainy finish and no marking on the back. (Often found with the "Made in Japan" sticker.) The reproduction quality is very poor, and easily spotted as "Not Hull" by collectors.

Louise Bauer, designer for Hull Pottery, personally designed the Gingergread line, including the Gingerbread Train Depot, which was introduced as a Limited Edition item by Larry Taylor in 1992. These Limited Edition issues are marked with the Hull imprint and the date of issue, so they are easily identified as new pieces.

Row 1:

#324	Child's Cup (Rare)
#801G	Train Depot, 9" x 6" x 11½" (Limited Edition/1992)
#325	Child's Bowl (Rare)

Row 2:

#123	Gingerbread Man Cookie Jar (Gray)
#399	Gingerbread Boy Coaster/Spoon Rest, 5"x5" (Brown)
#199	Gingerbread Boy Coaster/Spoon Rest, 5"x5" (Gray)

Row 3:

#198	Gingerbread Man Server, 10"x10" (Back Side)
#199	Crooksville State Bank imprint
#299	Crooksville State Bank imprint
#198	Gingerbread Man Server, 10"x10" (Brown)

The Gingerbread series continues to grow in popularity due to its broad range of collector appeal. The prices have more than doubled for these pieces over the last couple of years. The Child's Cup and Bowl are particularly rare and difficult to find.

See brochures featured under Accessories for other displays of the Gingerbread Man Cookie Jar, Spoon Rest and Servers on page 89. The Child's Cup and Bowl are also shown in the brochures displayed under Ring on page 94.

CENTENNIAL

The Centennial line was created for America's 1976 Bicentennial celebration. These molds are boldly imprinted with the American Bald Eagle. Production was limited, and in fact, it does not appear that the line was never marketed, so these pieces are quite difficult to find and priced accordingly.

Because these pieces were created as a collectible, most have never seen regular use and can often be found in mint condition. While the molds are very attractive, the curved handles on the casseroles, salt and pepper set, and the sugar bowl lend themselves to chipping and breaking by nature of their elongated design. Daily use is not recommended if you wish to retain the beauty and value of these pieces.

Row 1:

#573	Salt Shaker, 3" (Unmarked)
#585	Water/Milk Pitcher, 7½" (Unmarked)
#574	Pepper Shaker, 3" (Unmarked)

Row 2:

#572	Mug, 4" (Unmarked)
#586	Casserole w/cover, 4½" x 11"
#571	Cereal/Soup Bowl, 5¾" (Unmarked
	Star Decoration on Sides

Row 3:

#581	Creamer, 4½" (Unmarked)
#587	Bean Pot w/cover, 7" x 9"
#582	Sugar Bowl w/lid, 3¾"

These pieces are very difficult to price as the exact quantities produced has not been determined. Both artware and dinnerware collectors compete for these pieces, making them even more popular among Hull collectors.

Note: In the Imperial line a miniature bowl and pitcher set #F91 as displayed on page 114 also was imprinted with the American Bald Eagle. However, it is not considered a part of this set.

#584 Jumbo Mug, 32 oz.

House 'n Garden Serving-ware

an **OVENPROOF** *creation*

for casual living—

THE NEW AND FASHIONABLE WAY OF LIFE

Nationwide demand for the famous *Mirror Brown* continues to be sensational and the new additions are beyond comparison.

The significant Spread Eagle pattern appearing on several shapes is an American symbol implying strength and character which is consistent with ware expected to withstand constant daily use both in and out of doors. In combination with dinner and salad plates new starter sets are available.

Ceramically the line is prepared to endure oven heat, refrigeration, service in the breakfast nook, luncheon, the patio, barbecue, at the T.V. along with normal table service. Every piece is Dishwasher, Detergent and Oven Proof.

Imitations, by many manufacturers of ceramics are good . . . but *Originals* are better as evidenced by the unprecedented demands on our facilities.

 hull pottery company — crooksville, ohio *u.s.*

House 'n Garden Serving-ware

OVEN-PROOF

for the new way of life...

571 Fruit

572 Mug 12 oz.

573 Salt

574 Pepper

575 Salt & Pepper Set

581 Creamer

582 Sugar Bowl

583 Creamer & Sugar Set

584 Jumbo Stein 32 oz.

585 Pitcher 2 qt.

586 Casserole w/cover 4 pt.

587 Bean Pot 5 pt.

16 pc. Starter Set (Illustrated)
consisting of: 4 only #500 Dinner Plates
4 only #501 Salad Plates
4 only #571 Fruits
4 only #572 Mugs

Also Available:
12 pc. Starter Set
consisting of: 4 only #500 Dinner Plat
4 only #571 Fruits
4 only #572 Mugs

HULL POTTERY
CROOKSVILLE, OHIO

hull pottery company — crooksville. ohio *u.s.a.*

CENTERPIECES
Imperial Florist Ware & Miscellaneous

This section contains some of my favorite pieces. Most of the items in these pictures come from the Imperial Ware lines made for florists. There are so many molds and glazes to find in the Imperial lines, that I have only covered those that represent some of the more unusual and collectible pieces, and are avidly sought by dinnerware collectors.

The lovely fowl and animal molds make great centerpieces for your tables or decorations for your shelves, and come in an array of glazes to match your dinnerware sets. I use the Swan planter to serve spaghetti....and it's quite a conversation piece for my dinner guests!

Row 1:

#F445	Candle Holders (Pair) (Butterscotch)	
#815I	Swan Ash Tray (Butterscotch)	
#F88	Sculptured Pedestal Planter (Brown)	

Row 2:

#F70	Caricature Frog (Brown) (Hard to Find)	
#F1	Bud Vase (Brown)	
#F70	Caricature Frog (Dk Green) (Hard to Find)	

Row 3:

#F71	Swan Planter (Butterscotch)*	
#F71	Swan Planter (Tangerine)	
#F71	Swan Planter (Brown)	

*The Swans are especially coveted by collectors and are extremely hard to find in the colored glazes. Also found in Country Squire green agate and white.

Row 4:

#F68	Caricature Hippo Planter (Brown)	
#F69	Duck Planter (Brown)	
#F68	Caricature Hippo Planter (Dk Green)	

The Swan, Duck and Hippo planters are listed in the following brochures as Hull's Aquatic Animals and were manufactured during the late 70's and early 80's. However, the Swan was originally manufactured in the 60's as #F812 in Satin White only.

The Imperial Ware molds were glazed in a number of colors, however, most were finished in dark green, white and brown. The brighter colors such as butterscotch and tangerine are rare and highly prized.

Most molds are easily identified by their factory assigned number and the Hull imprint; however, I often run across pieces that I am not able to identify but feel the weights, glazes and other markings indicate that they are Hull Pottery products. Those pieces in this plate picture that I can't verify are Hull and are marked accordingly. While I cannot with any authority state that they are Hull items, I am still delighted to have them in my collection, particularly because they make great additions to my Tangerine dinnerware set!

Row 1:

#F91	Eagle Pitcher Set
#F478	Round Centerpiece Ped. Flower Bowl
#F91	Eagle Pitcher in Dark Green

Row 2:

#890I	Pedestal Flower Bowl (Unmarked)
#F61	Heart-Shaped Garden Dish
#891I	Rectangular Footed Flower Dish (Unmarked)

Row 3:

#F35	Cylindrical Vase
#F63	Imperial Leaf (Note inside detail)
#892I	Long Stem Vase (Unmarked)

Row 4:

#A50	Rose Pitcher
#B6	Fancy Ruffled Bowl
#F90	Single Bud Vase
#893I	Candy Dish/Centerpiece

The following brochures contain many more pieces from the Imperial ware line that are especially delightful to find, such as the handled baskets and embossed planters.

The brochure on page 116 listed these items as available in satin white, jade green and wild honey! Notice the bold and unusual shapes of the planters and vases in these pictures.

Hull collectors are just now taking notice of the Imperial planters and vases. These pieces were made by the thousands and distributed throughout the U.S. as florist dishes. The standard rectangular pieces in dark green are very common and can be found easily. The embellished pieces are more collectible and valuable.

Vases — Planters
Flower Bowls

Imperial Ware

SW—Satin White
JG—Jade Green
WH—Wild Honey

F401
Low Round Flower Bowl
6" Dia. x 3"

F410
Pedestaled Flower Bowl
6" Dia. x 4¾"

F411
Square Footed Planter
5½" x 4¾" Hi.

F412
Urn Planter
5¼" Dia. x 5"

F416
Bell Vase
10"

F422
Oriental Planter
6¾" x 4½" x 2¼"

F425
Octagonal Compote
7½" x 4¼"

F430
Footed Round Flower Bowl
5¾" Dia. x 4" Hi. x 3½"
opening

F432
Chalice Vase
8¾"

F433
Pedestaled Ivy Vase
10"

F434
Urn Vase
7"

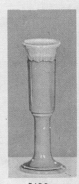

F435
Bud Vase
9"

F445
Candle Holder
4½" Hi.

F436
Float Bowl Console
11" x 8" x 1¾"

F445
Candle Holder
4½" Hi.

F439
Usubata Vase
8½"

 Hull Pottery Company -- Crooksville, Ohio

Some additional items from the Imperial line that are especially colorful or unusual are the Imperial Leaf Dishes shown on the following pages.

Picture 1:
#F63   Leaf Dish (Tangerine with gold decoration.)

Picture 2:
#F63   Leaf Dish (Cobalt Blue)
Many feel that the experimental cobalt blue dinnerware found in the House 'n Garden molds was finished with this glaze....which was also used with the Continental artware.

Picture 3:
#F48   Small (5" x 2¾") Planter.
(This planter has been found in Tangerine also.)

Picture 4:
#1018M   Experimental Bud Vase:
This vase is clearly an adaptation of the F433 Pedestaled Ivy Vase shown in the brochure on page 116. The mold was turned upside-down and the base was removed...with a new base attached. This was an exciting find!

Picture 5:
#F71   Swan Centerpiece in Country Squire/Green Agate

#815I   Swan Ash Tray in Country Squire/Green Agate

Picture 6:
#894I   Circle H Basketweave Planter, 4" high.

Picture 7:
#895I   Bunny Candy Dish (Rare)

Picture 8:
#896I   Fan Vase in Country Squire/Green Agate.

Picture 9:
#897I   Pair of matching Footed Vases in Tangerine with Green Foam trim.
(Note: Front side lower than back.)

PICTURE 1

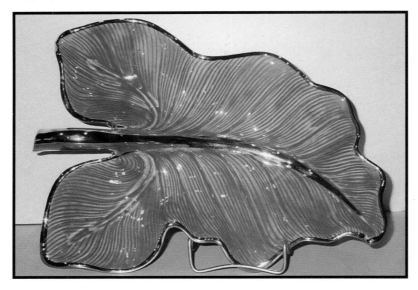

PICTURE 2

PICTURE 3

PICTURE 4

PICTURE 5

PICTURE 7

PICTURE 6

PICTURE 8

PICTURE 9

Food for thought.

Hull's Garden Dishes grace table settings two ways, not only as functional planters but also as attractive garnish and snack bowls. That's an appetizing thought for your customers!

† F77 Fancy Oval Garden Dish
11½" × 5¼" × 3"

† A6 Scroll Flower Dish
9" × 5½" × 3⅛"

† F41 Rect. Low Flower Bowl
7½" × 5½" × 2¼"

* F61 Heart-Shaped Garden Dish
7" × 3" High

† Best-Selling Carry-Over Items
* New Items

(Knives and flowers not included)

*F66

F66 Oval Handled Basket
7" × 7" High

* F67 Wicker Embossed Handled Basket
7½" Long × 8" High

Baskets are always best sellers!
Richly embossed floral and wicker patterns make them outstanding complements to every arrangement. Like the entire Imperial line, they are available in deep green, warm brown or satiny white to give them instant and long-lasting appeal.

† B36 Footed Basket
7" Diameter × 9" High

(Flowers and Macrame not included)

† F469 Paneled Garden Dish
7¾'' × 4¾'' × 3¼''

† F75 Garden Dish
6½'' × 3⅞'' × 2¾''

† Best-Selling Carry-Over Items
* New Items

† F467 Fluted Garden Dish
7'' × 4½'' × 3''

† F76 Garden Dish
7'' × 4'' × 3⅛''

† F17 Daisy Embossed Garden Dish
7¾'' × 4¾'' × 3¼''

† F18 Fruit Embossed Garden Dish
8¾'' × 4¾'' × 3¼''

123

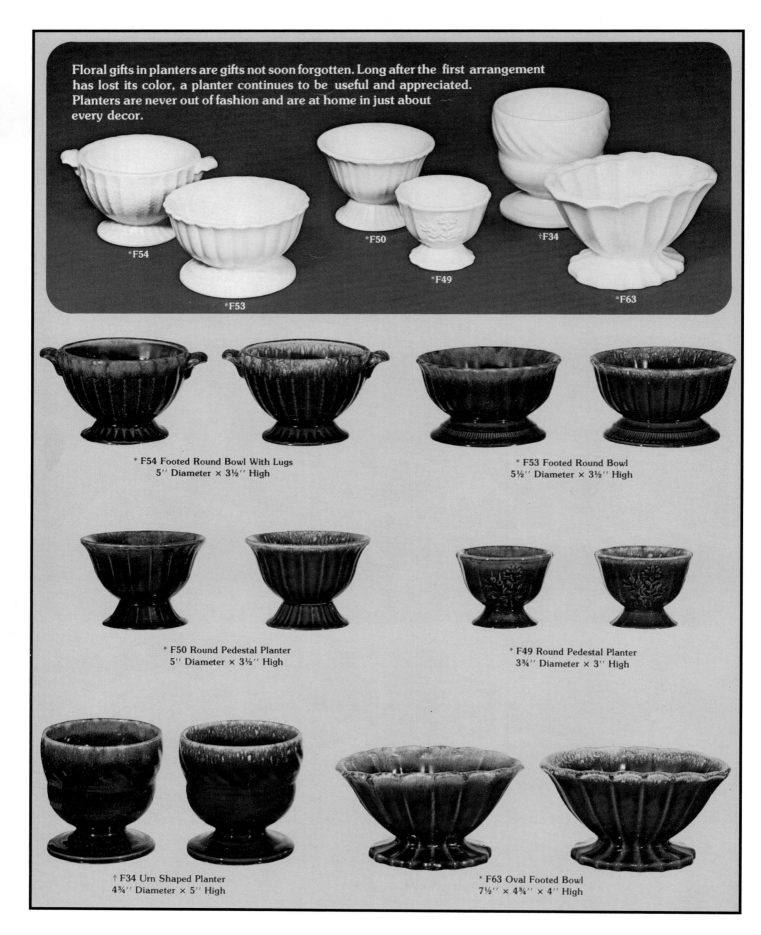

Floral gifts in planters are gifts not soon forgotten. Long after the first arrangement has lost its color, a planter continues to be useful and appreciated. Planters are never out of fashion and are at home in just about every decor.

*F54

*F53

*F50

*F49

†F34

*F63

* F54 Footed Round Bowl With Lugs
5'' Diameter × 3½'' High

* F53 Footed Round Bowl
5½'' Diameter × 3½'' High

* F50 Round Pedestal Planter
5'' Diameter × 3½'' High

* F49 Round Pedestal Planter
3¾'' Diameter × 3'' High

† F34 Urn Shaped Planter
4¾'' Diameter × 5'' High

* F63 Oval Footed Bowl
7½'' × 4¾'' × 4'' High

Be imaginative!

Create your own atmosphere with our planters. Choose the style and color you want. Hard-to-arrange florals will always look their best in Imperial pottery.

† F5 Swirl Goblet Planter
4¾'' High

† F88 Sculptured Pedestal Planter
5¼'' × 5⅜''

* F56 Footed Six-Sided Planter
5'' × 5'' High

* F55 Footed Six-Sided Planter
5¼'' × 3¼''

* F62 Eight-Sided Footed Bowl
7'' × 3¾'' High

† A54 Round Pedestal Planter
4'' Diameter Top × 5'' High

† Best-Selling Carry-Over Items
* New Items

(Floral arrangements not included)

† I-21 Oval Fluted Garden Dish
8″ × 5½″ × 3″

* F60 Round Paneled Bowl
7″ Diameter × 3¼″ High

† B6 Fancy Ruffled Bowl
7⅝″ × 3¾″ High

* F59 Round Paneled Bowl
6″ Diameter × 3¼″ High

Many items in the Imperial line are ideal for hanging baskets but take special note that we do **not** furnish the macrame commonly used for hanging basket purposes. The two items F65 and F66 illustrated as hanging baskets show only their adaptable usage, the same as illustrated flowers and vegetables.

† F10 Fluted Round Flower Bowl
6½″ Diameter × 3¾″ High

F65 Embossed Round Bowl
6″ Diameter × 3½″ High

126

† A2 Square Footed Planter
5'' Square × 3½'' High

* F58 Vase With Flared Top
5¼'' High

Designed for you.

Whether formal or casual, our varied selection of shapes and colors lets you meet all your customers' needs. That will mean greater satisfaction for them and increased sales for you.

* F64 Oval Vase
6½'' High

† Best-Selling Carry-Over Items
* New Items

† F404 Footed Garden Dish
7'' × 4'' × 3''

† F405 Footed Flower Dish
8¼'' × 4½'' × 3¼''

† F78 Rectangular Leaf Design Garden Dish
10½'' × 5¼'' × 3⅜''

† F47 Rectangular Garden Dish
11¾'' × 4¾'' × 4''

† F447 Paneled Garden Dish
6¼'' × 4'' × 2⅜''

* F52 Footed Planter
7'' × 4¾'' × 3¼'' High

† B34 Footed Garden Dish
9½'' × 5¼'' × 4½'' High

* F48 Small Planter
5'' × 2¾'' × 2½'' High

* F51 Three Footed Pot
4¼'' Diameter × 4½'' High

* F57 Square Footed Planter
4¾'' × 4¾'' High

The Imperial line has been the florist's choice for years. Its strength of design has enabled it to bridge the ever-turning tide of fad and fashion. If you want pottery that's always accepted, you'll buy Imperial.

*F57

†B34

* New Items
† Best-Selling Carry-Over Items

* F70 Caricature Frog
7'' Wide × 6½'' High

* F68 Caricature Hippo Planter
8½'' Long × 5'' Wide × 4¼'' High

Hull's Aquatic Animals

Our aquatic animals will be pets in any setting. Their cheerful presence is perfect for rec-rooms, centerpieces or informal arrangements.

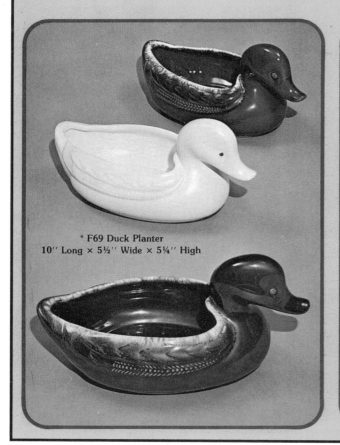

* F69 Duck Planter
10'' Long × 5½'' Wide × 5¼'' High

* F71 Swan
9'' Long × 5½'' Wide × 8'' High

The Imperial Line offers a large variety of shapes and the three most popular underglaze color combinations which may be mixed in cartons at no extra cost. But the total quantities per carton as indicated in our price list remain standard.

Imperial by Hull

† F39 Fluted Oval Garden Dish
7″ × 4¼″ × 2¼″

† F83 Pressed Pedestal Planter
6″ Diameter × 3½″ High

† F42 Rectangular Fluted Garden Dish
8½″ × 5″ × 3¼″

† Best-Selling Carry-Over Items
(Florals not included)

MISCELLANEOUS & TEST PIECES

Because the workers at the Hull plant were encouraged to be creative, many employee specials and test pieces are often found by collectors. The items on the following page represent a sampling of the unusual pieces I have found over the years, and other miscellaneous items.

Note: Dinnerware in a dark (cobalt) blue has been discovered in a very limited quantity. While I have seen a few of these pieces, I do not have any examples for publication. This note is to alert dinnerware collectors of the existence of this employee special glaze.

I have included the coffee pot, cups and casserole below that were produced prior to the 1960's introduction of the House 'n Garden lines. The coffee pot mold is identical to the one used in the House 'n Garden line. The casserole also was produced in a pink glaze with black trim on the bottom.

#897M Coffee Cup
#898M Coffee Pot
#899M Casserole w/cover

(These pieces are listed in the value guide under Miscellaneous.)

#890M

#891M

The handled casserole and covered bowl above are also from the line produced during the 1950's. These pieces are usually heavier than the House 'n Garden. Most are marked with the "Hull" imprint.

Row 1:
   Test Cups   Used to test glaze finishes
   Creamer   Bright yellow glaze w/brown trim
   Coffee Cup, 9 Oz.   Gray with white decal
   Coffee Cup, 7 Oz.   Unusual tan/brown glaze

Row 2:
   Mushroom S&P
     Sets   Cream with brown drip trim
                      Mirror Almond
   Coffee Cup   Heartland with flower decal
   Blue Bowl   Probably from an earlier line

Note: These pieces are not included in the value guide.

These pieces are from the collection of Lori Friend of Statesville, North Carolina. Lori and her husband, Steve, are avid Hull Pottery collectors of both the artware and dinnerware lines.

Picture 1 & 2: (Front and Back)
  #1001M   Ash Tray w/ 8 Sides
           Marked A-5
           Probably a test piece in Mirror Brown

Picture 3:
  #1002M   Mug, 9 Oz.
           Imprint: "Purdue University"

Picture 4:
  #1003M   Beer Stein, 16 Oz.
           Imprint: "Tremont Nail Company"

Picture 5:
  #1004M   Bean Pot, 2 Qt.
           Imprint: "Boston Baked Beans"
           Probably employee special

Many imprinted and specialized items can be found in the dinnerware pieces. Especially in the coffee mugs and beer steins. These unusual items are usually priced about 25% higher, and are sought by collectors for their unique markings.

These pieces are listed in the value guide under Miscellaneous.

This picture of the Sitting Pig Bank is from Cindy Mountz of Elverson, PA. Many of these pigs imprinted with "The 1982 World's Fair Knoxville, Tennessee" can be found. The imprint has been found on beer steins and 10 oz. Mugs.

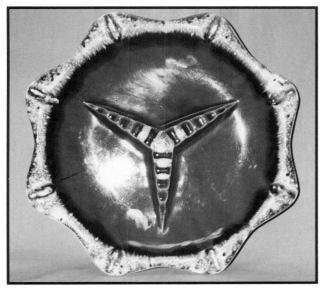

PICTURE 1 (front)

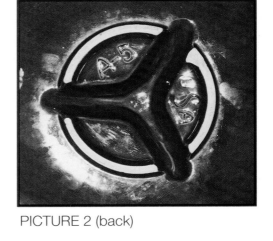

PICTURE 2 (back)

PICTURE 3

PICTURE 4

PICTURE 5

Picture 6 & 7:
#1005M   (Butterscotch & Avocado 16 Oz. Steins)
      "Academia/Batesina Condita 1864"
      "University of Illinois Chartered 1867"

Picture 8 & 9:
#1006M   (Mirror Brown & Gray Continental Mugs)
      "The 1982 World's Fair"
      "3rd Annual Convention/American Art Pottery Association"

Picture 10:
#1007M   Test Cups (Country Squire/Tangerine/Mirror Brown/Imperial
      Dark Green)
      (Used to test glaze finishes.)

Picture 11:
#1008M   Experimental Ash Tray (Mirror Brown)

Picture 12:
#1009M   Heart-Shaped Ash Tray (Unusual Lavender Glaze)

Picture 13:
#1010M   Souffle Dish (Country Squire/Green Agate)
      As the mold was issued after Country Squire, this piece is a special
      find for collectors.

PICTURE 6

PICTURE 7

PICTURE 8

PICTURE 9

PICTURE 10

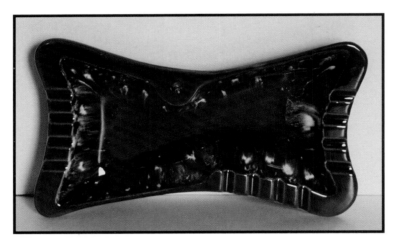

PICTURE 11

PICTURE 12

PICTURE 13

Picture 14:
      #1011M   Experimental Pitcher (Mirror Brown)
                       This beautiful 1960's piece is decorated with raised orchids and is
                       from Lori Friend's collections. (Rare).

Picture 15:
      #1012M   Hull Plaque: This 1992 piece was a special offer Limited Edition by
                       the Ohio Pottery Museum during the pottery festival.

Picture 16:
      #1013M   Unknown Turtle Planter: The origins of this piece and the Fish
                       Planter below has not been confirmed, however, they are a trea-
                       sured part of my collection and I am still researching hoping to find
                       that they are Hull experimental pieces!

Picture 17:
      #1014M   Unknown Fish Planter

Picture 18:
      #1015M   #F473 Imperial Chickadee Planter in Mirror Brown
                       (This is an unusual glaze for this piece.)

Picture 19:
      #1016M   Divided Server, late 1980's in Mirror Brown, 11"

Picture 20:
      #1017M   1950's Cook 'n Serve handled skillet in Mirror Brown

PICTURE 14

PICTURE 15

PICTURE 16

PICTURE 17

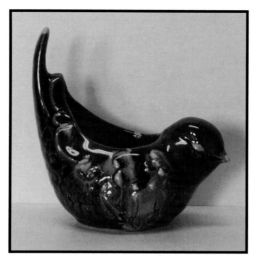

PICTURE 18

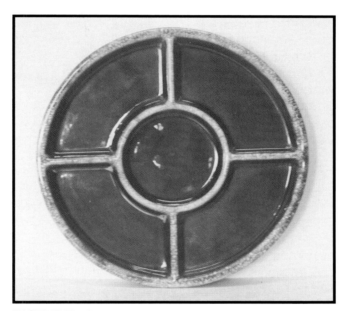

PICTURE 19

PICTURE 20

HULL'S DESIGNER & MODELER

Little recognition has been given to Louise Bauer of Zanesville, Ohio who was Hull's principal designer and modeler from 1949 to the close of the pottery in 1985. Prior to her tenure with Hull, Ms. Bauer previously worked as an independent designer for several prominent potteries. Among those were the Leeds China Company, Royal China and Royal Manufacturing where she designed many of Disney's pottery figurines which are so collectible today. Her work included many of the figural cookie jars, banks, salt and pepper sets and planters in Disney's popular cartoon characters, Mickey & Minnie, Donald Duck and Cinderella. Other well-known pottery companies that contracted for her design work along with Hull were Shawnee Pottery of Ohio, American Bisque of Pennsylvania, and Western Stoneware of Illinois. In fact, Ms. Bauer designed Western's Mar-Crest dinnerware which is another prevalent dinnerware line among pottery dinnerware collectibles. This line was produced in a dark brown glaze, imprinted with a simple star and flower design and produced in numerous serving and dinnerware molds.

It was through her work with Western Stoneware that Mr. A.E. Hull came to contact Ms. Bauer to do some design work for the Hull Pottery after their designer, Eva Zeisel, resigned and returned to New York. Mr. Hull had close ties with Western Stoneware at the time and was familiar with Ms. Bauer's design work. When Eva Zeisel left before her work was completed, he called in Louise Bauer to complete the unfinished line. This line was one of Hull's most popular and was named Bow-Knot and today is recognized by artware and dinnerware collectors alike. Mr. Hull was so pleased with her work that he asked her to stay on to design another line. Her first complete line for Hull Pottery was the popular Woodland series.

One of Ms. Bauer's fondest memories involved the presentation of a Best of Show award for her 1955 Ebb Tide design. The award was presented at a dinner held at the Pittsburgh Show in Pennsylvania, and according to Ms. Bauer, it was quite an exciting award to receive considering the fact that Mr. Hull was "so persnickety" about the designs! Hull's reputation in the pottery market was a source of pride for Mr. Hull, and he demanded new and unique designs to retain Hull's recognition in the pottery world.

She continued with Hull Pottery, acting as their exclusive designer for nearly 40 years, and was responsible for the many artware and novelty wares produced throughout her tenure with the company. Her designs included the Imperial florist ware line and most of Hull's House 'n Garden dinnerware lines which are the subject of this book.

Not only did she produce the lines of drawing form, but she also was required to cast a model of each piece, which was not an easy task; requiring extensive clay and plaster work. To accommodate the space and materials needed, Ms. Bauer maintained a workshop at her home, crafting the various molds until a suitable model could be produced to present to the pottery for casting. Sometimes the models had to be reworked to meet the requirements of Hull's casters. If a mold was too difficult to extract from a cast, or contained details too small or complicated to achieve a good reproduction, then adjustments in the mold were required until a cast could be produced that met production requirements.

These molds were often heavy and cumbersome, especially the larger pieces. And the efforts to create a three dimensional mold from a drawing required a great deal of artistic talent. But Ms. Bauer had both the talent and the wherewithal to accomplish this feat over and over again as evidenced by the many beautiful and functional pieces that were created in her workshop!

Among her favorite lines are Hull's Centennial, which never experienced full production, and the Gingerbread line. Ms. Bauer is still in possession of her original drawings for the Gingerbread Train Canister Set.

Among her most popular designs were the House 'n Garden Chicken and Duck casseroles. The animals and fowl shaped serving pieces were her ideas transformed into usable kitchenware. Her particular specialty was the ability to create these unusual animal shaped serving dishes which are the badge of Hull's House 'n Garden line. The style and features of these lovable pieces are easily identified by collectors. Her experience working on the "Disney" lines is undoubtedly reflected in the caricature representations of these molds.

Ms. Bauer still resides in Mt. Sterling, Ohio with her sister at their family home. She is always delighted to talk about her years with Hull Pottery and is a wealth of information about the pottery's 40 year history prior to its closure. Ms. Bauer is shown here in a 1992 photograph proudly wearing her "Hull" sweatshirt. Like Louise, it's a one-of-a-kind...that only she could produce.

A TRIP TO CROOKSVILLE

For the past several years, my family and I have made annual trips to Crooksville on buying excursions. Each year we return exhausted, but elated over some new and special find.

I was so excited to finally reach Crooksville after years of dreaming of making a trip, that my husband took this picture so that I would always remember that moment when we reached our destination!

Our first trip was the most exciting because it was the first time I saw the Hull plant. The first thing we did when we arrived in Crooksville was to locate the factory...again another picture to remember the event!

No trip to Crooksville is complete without a trip to the Ohio Pottery Museum.

My husband, Bill, looking at the displays. Note the Hull greenware in the workshop at the museum. (This greenware was obtained at the auction when the pottery was closed.)

These pieces were finished and glazed and offered for sale by the museum. At the time of this photograph, these pieces were not marked to indicate that they were finished at the museum; however, since that time, these pieces have been marked or signed by the finishers.

Shopping in the many antique malls and shops in the area is, of course, one of the main events of trips. It's a Hull Collector's fantasy come true.

Just look at the shelves full of Hull Pottery dinnerware and artware. Nowhere else can you find such an array of Hull, except during the Pottery Festival in July.

Exhausted and broke, we always record our "finds" on film so that we can relive the trip and the excitement again and again. Bill found his starter set in the Ridge gray on this trip...and the Gingerbread man cookie jar...that was the end of his passive interest in my hobby; he was "hooked." We call these pictures our "Haul of Hull."

SPECIAL MUSEUM PRODUCTIONS

These pieces represent some of the unfinished molds that were handpainted by Nancy Dennis of the Ohio Pottery Museum. These beautiful pieces are from the collection of Joan Gray Hull.

No value has been listed in the value guide for these pieces, as they are not Hull production items, and, I do not consider myself qualified to price these unique and beautiful works of art! Nancy Dennis' talent is apparent in the wonderful designs and landscape scenes painted on these Hull molds, which were some of the final molds taken from the Hull Pottery Company at its closure.

VALUE GUIDE

This book is only intended as a guide for the collector. The values indicated are not intended to establish prices for the market, but to create a guideline. Prices vary from one section of the country to the other depending on interest, quantity, and quality. I have determined the current values represented in this book by averaging both selling and buying prices from both collectors and dealers from all areas of the country. Neither I, nor the publisher, takes any responsibility for losses incurred as a result of using this guide.

In order to reference the value guide for easy use, I have separated the dinnerware pieces into their various lines and listed each item by its production number in ascending order. If no number was available, I have assigned one for reference. All numbers that have been assigned for the purposes of producing this guide end with the first letter of the dinnerware line, i.e. the Gingerbread Train Canister Set has been assigned the number 801G, the Gingerbread Train Depot has been assigned the number 802G, etc.

To locate a price in the guide, simply note the dinnerware line and the assigned number. In the index, locate the dinnerware line by name, (dinnerware lines are listed in alphabetical order) and the assigned number is listed below in ascending order. Also, to assist new collectors, glazes (colors) are also referenced along with the dinnerware line name.

While this is not the standard format for Collector Books, I felt that it provides a quicker reference for the collectors utilizing this guide, and was possible due to the fact that so many brochures indicating factory assigned numbers were available.
I have found that locating a particular piece using this method is quicker and easier than listing the items by page, row, and plate number.

In addition to the plate pictures, all brochure items (with the exception of sets) are listed. Set values can be determined by summing the value of the individual pieces in a set. However, if you are lucky enough to find a set, you can expect to pay more than the individual book values; especially if the set is in mint condition and still in the original box!

In a few instances, the factory assigned number appears more than once under the House 'n Garden and Imperial lines. This is due to the fact that the factory reused numbers when molds were retired. However, there are only a few of these duplicates, and the items are easily identified by their descriptions.

Note: The Imperial pricing reflects pricing for all glazes, regardless of color, unless otherwise noted.

ACCESSORY (GRAY)

No.	Description	Value
102	Mug, 10 Oz.	$3.00-5.00
114	Round Casserole w/cover	$14.00-18.00
160	Canister Set, 4-Piece Stacking	$90.00-110.00
176	Custard Cup, 8 Oz.	$5.00-7.00
1195	Corky Pig Bank	$50.00-60.00
1196	Sitting Pig Bank	$50.00-60.00
1505	Garlic Cellar, 13 Oz.	$15.00-20.00
1507	Casserole w/lid, 32 Oz.	$22.00-26.00
1509	Water Jug, 5 Pt., 80 Oz.	$18.00-25.00
1510	Bean Pot w/cover, 2 Qt.	$22.00-26.00
1513	Fr. Handle Indv. Casserole/Open, 12 Oz.	$5.00-7.00
1514	Ice Jug, 2 Qt.	$18.00-25.00
1518	Creamer or Jug, 8 Oz. (10 Oz.)	$5.00-7.00
1522	Coffee Pot, 8 Cup	$35.00-45.00
1523	Cookie Jar w/cover, 94 Oz.	$35.00-45.00
1524	Indv. Bean Pot w/cover, 12 Oz.	$10.00-12.00
1525	Jug, 2 Pt.	$20.00-30.00
1526	Beer Stein, 16 Oz.	$9.00-12.00
1527	Fr. Handle Indv. Casserole w/cover, 12 Oz.	$9.00-12.00
1535	Onion Soup Bowl w/cover, 12 Oz.	$10.00-12.00
1536	Mixing Bowl, 6"	$8.00-12.00
1537	Mixing Bowl, 7"	$9.00-15.00
1538	Mixing Bowl, 8"	$12.00-16.00
1544	Oval Casserole w/cover, 2 Pt.	$20.00-25.00
1545	Salad or Spaghetti Bowl, 10¼"	$18.00-24.00
1548	Oval Casserole w/cover, 2 Qt.	$22.00-28.00
1549	Tea Pot w/cover, 5 Cup	$22.00-28.00
1550	Jam/Mustard Jar w/cover, 13 Oz.	$12.00-14.00
1553	Soup Mug, 11 Oz.	$6.00-8.00
1554	Tray for Snack Set	$7.00-10.00
1561	Covered Butter Dish, ¼ lb.	$12.00-15.00
1566	Pie Plate, 9¼" Dia.	$16.00-22.00
1568	Square Baker, 3 Pt.	$8.00-12.00
1569	Soup or Salad Bowl, 6½"	$5.00-7.00
1571	Continental Mug, 10 Oz.	$10.00-12.00
1573	Oval Bake 'n Serve Dish, 9½ Oz.	$7.00-9.00
1574	Oval Bake 'n Serve Dish, 16 Oz.	$7.00-9.00
1581	Indv. Oval Spaghetti, 10¾"x 8¼"	$12.00-14.00
1589	Bake 'n Serve, 6½", Round	$5.00-7.00
1595	Handled Skillet, 18 Oz.	$16.00-20.00
1600	2½ Oz. Ramekin	$6.00-7.00
15280	Oval Casserole w/Duck cover, 2 Pt	$55.00-70.00
15850	Oval Casserole w/Chicken cover, 2 Qt.	$55.00-70.00

ACCESSORY (SAND)

No.	Description	Value
202	Mug, 10 Oz.	$3.00-5.00
214	Round Casserole w/cover	$14.00-18.00
260	Canister Set, 4-Piece Stacking	$90.00-110.00
276	Custard Cup, 8 Oz.	$5.00-7.00
2195	Corky Pig Bank	$50.00-60.00
2196	Sitting Pig Bank	$50.00-60.00
2505	Garlic Cellar, 13 Oz.	$15.00-20.00
2507	Casserole w/lid, 32 Oz.	$16.00-22.00
2509	Water Jug, 5 Pt., 80 Oz.	$18.00-25.00
2510	Bean Pot w/cover, 2 Qt.	$12.00-26.00
2513	Fr. Handle Indv. Casserole/Open, 12 Oz.	$5.00-7.00
2514	Ice Jug, 2 Qt.	$15.00-25.00
2518	Creamer or Jug, 8 Oz., (10 Oz.)	$5.00-7.00
2522	Coffee Pot, 8 Cup	$35.00-45.00
2523	Cookie Jar w/cover, 94 Oz.	$35.00-45.00
2524	Indv. Bean Pot w/cover, 12 Oz.	$10.00-12.00
2525	Jug, 2 Pt.	$20.00-30.00
2526	Beer Stein, 16 Oz.	$9.00-12.00
2527	Fr. Handle Indv. Casserole w/cover, 12 Oz.	$9.00-12.00
2535	Onion Soup Bowl w/Cover, 12 Oz.	$10.00-12.00
2536	Mixing Bowl, 6"	$8.00-12.00
2537	Mixing Bowl, 7"	$9.00-15.00
2538	Mixing Bowl, 8"	$12.00-16.00
2544	Oval Casserole w/cover, 2 Pt.	$20.00-25.00
2545	Salad or Spaghetti Bowl, 10¼"	$18.00-24.00
2548	Oval Casserole w/cover, 2 Qt.	$22.00-28.00
2549	Tea Pot w/cover, 5 Cup	$22.00-28.00
2550	Jam/Mustard Jar w/cover, 13 Oz.	$12.00-14.00
2553	Soup Mug, 11 Oz.	$6.00-8.00
2554	Tray for Snack Set	$7.00-10.00
2561	Covered Butter Dish, ¼ lb.	$12.00-15.00
2566	Pie Plate, 9¼" Dia.	$16.00-22.00
2568	Square Baker, 3 Pt.	$8.00-12.00
2569	Soup or Salad Bowl, 6½"	$5.00-7.00
2571	Continental Mug, 10 Oz.	$10.00-12.00
2573	Oval Bake 'n Serve Dish, 9½ Oz.	$7.00-9.00
2574	Oval Bake 'n Serve Dish, 16 Oz.	$7.00-9.00
2581	Indv. Oval Spaghetti, 10¾" x 8¼"	$12.00-14.00
2589	Bake 'n Serve, 6½" Round	$5.00-7.00
2595	Handled Skillet, 18 Oz.	$16.00-20.00
2600	2½ Oz. Ramekin	$6.00-7.00
25280	Oval Casserole w/Duck cover, 2 Pt.	$55.00-70.00
25850	Oval Casserole w/Chicken cover, 2 Qt.	$55.00-70.00

ACCESSORY BROWN

(See House 'n Garden/Mirror Brown)

AVOCADO

No.	Description	Value
600	Dinner Plate, 10¼"	$6.00-8.00
601	Salad Plate, 6½"	$4.00-5.00
602	Coffee Cup (Mug), 9 Oz.	$4.00-5.00
603	Fruit Bowl, 5¼"	$3.00-5.00
610	Bean Pot w/cover, 2 Qt.	$22.00-28.00
613	Fr. Handle Indv. Casserole/Open, 12 Oz.	$4.00-5.00
615	Salt Shaker w/cork, 3¾"	$4.00-6.00
616	Pepper Shaker w/cork, 3¾"	$4.00-6.00
618	Creamer or Jug, 8 Oz.	$7.00-9.00
619	Sugar Bowl w/cover, 12 Oz.	$7.00-9.00
621	Chip 'n Dip Leaf, 15" x 10½"	$25.00-35.00
622	Coffee Pot w/cover, 8 Cup	$32.00-40.00
624	Indv. Bean Pot w/cover, 12 Oz.	$7.00-9.00
625	Jug, 2 Pt.	$18.00-25.00
626	Beer Stein, 16 Oz.	$6.00-8.00
627	Fr. Handle Indv. Casserole w/cover, 12 Oz.	$6.00-7.00
633	Fruit Bowl, 6"	$4.00-6.00
635A	Rectangular Roaster w/cover, 7 Pt.	$55.00-65.00
641	Indv. Oval Steak Plate, 11¾" x 9"	$8.00-12.00
642	Divided Vegetable Dish, 10¾" x 7¼"	$8.00-12.00
648	Oval Casserole w/cover, 2 Qt.	$22.00-26.00
649	Tea Pot w/cover, 5 cup	$20.00-25.00
651	Jam/Mustard Jar w/cover, 12 Oz.	$7.00-9.00
661	Covered Butter Dish, ¼ lb.	$8.00-10.00
666	Pie Plate, 9¼" Dia.	$16.00-22.00
669	Soup or Salad Bowl, 6½"	$5.00-7.00
674	Oval Bake 'n Serve Dish, 16 Oz.	$6.00-8.00
687A	Salt Shaker/Mushroom, 3¾"	$12.00-15.00
688A	Pepper Shaker/Mushroom, 3¾"	$12.00-15.00
689A	Gravy Boat w/tray	$60.00-80.00
690A	Chip 'n Dip (6 Sides) Set	$80.00-100.00
697	Coffee Cup, 7 Oz.	$4.00-6.00
698	Saucer, 5⅞"	$3.00-4.00
699	Luncheon Plate, 9⅜"	$7.00-9.00

CENTENNIAL
(Brown)

No.	Description	Value
571	Cereal Bowl, 5¾" (Unmarked)	$40.00-50.00
572	Mug, 4" (Unmarked)	$40.00-50.00
573	Salt Shaker, 3" (Unmarked)	$26.00-30.00
574	Pepper Shaker, 3" (Unmarked)	$26.00-30.00
581	Creamer, 4½" (Unmarked)	$40.00-50.00
582	Sugar Bowl, 3¾"	$40.00-50.00
584	Stein, (32 Oz.)	$45.00-55.00
585	Milk Pitcher, 7½" (Unmarked)	$90.00-110.00
586	Casserole, 4½" x 11"	$90.00-110.00
587	Bean Pot w/cover, 7" x 9"	$90.00-110.00

COUNTRY BELLE
(White/Blue Flower/Bell Stencil)

No.	Description	Value
6400	Dinner Plate	$9.00-12.00
6401	Salad Plate	$6.00-8.00
6402	Coffee Cup	$6.00-7.00
6403	Soup/Salad Bowl, 12 Oz.	$7.00-9.00
6405	Saucer for Coffee Cup	$5.00-6.00
6408	Oval Serving Bowl	$16.00-22.00
6410	Bean Pot w/cover	$25.00-35.00
6418	Creamer	$10.00-15.00
6419	Sugar Bowl	$12.00-16.00
6422	Gravy Boat w/tray	$22.00-28.00
6423	Cookie Jar	$38.00-48.00
6425	Dessert Plate	$7.00-9.00
6428	Round Casserole w/cover	$30.00-40.00
6436	Bowl, 6"	$12.00-18.00
6438	Bowl, 8"	$15.00-22.00
6440	Bowl, 10"	$22.00-26.00
6441	Oval Platter	$22.00-25.00
6442	Soup/Salad Bowl, 20 Oz.	$9.00-11.00
6444	Quiche Dish	$18.00-28.00
6449	Coffee Pot	$40.00-50.00
6452	Sugar/Creamer Set	$17.00-21.00
6453	Salt & Pepper Set w/handles	$25.00-32.00
6462	Unlabeled Condiment Server	$15.00-18.00
6466	Round Baker/Cobbler Dish	$22.00-28.00
6470	Pitcher, 36 Oz.	$35.00-40.00
6471	Stemmed Coffee Cup	$8.00-10.00
6472	Pitcher, 66 Oz.	$42.00-57.00
6473	109 Oz. Bowl/FOR BOW L & PITCHER	$35.00-45.00
6476	Custard Cup	$6.00-8.00
6490	Canister Set	$125.00-170.00
6517	Souffle Dish	$25.00-29.00
6567	Rectangular Baker	$28.00-32.00
6568	Square Baker	$14.00-18.00
6595	Handled Skillet	$22.00-28.00
65280	Oval Casserole w/Duck cover, 2 Pt.	$55.00-70.00
65850	Oval Casserole w/Chicken cover, 2 Qt.	$55.00-70.00

COUNTRY SQUIRE
(Green Agate)

No.	Description	Value
100	Dinner Plate, 10¼"	$7.00-9.00
101	Salad Plate, 6½"	$4.00-5.00
102	Coffee Cup, (Mug) 9 Oz.	$5.00-6.00
103	Fruit Bowl, 5¼"	$3.00-5.00
105	Mixing Bowl, 5¼"	$8.00-10.00

COUNTRY SQUIRE (Continued)
(Green Agate)

No.	Description	Value
106	Mixing Bowl, 6¾"	$9.00-12.00
107	Mixing Bowl, 8¼"	$12.00-15.00
109	Water Jug 5 Pt., 80 Oz.	$28.00-32.00
110	Bean Pot w/cover, 2 Qt.	$22.00-28.00
111	Bake/Casserole Dish, 3 Pt.	$12.00-15.00
112	Bake/Casserole Dish, 3 Pt. w/cover	$18.00-22.00
113	Fr. Handle Indv. Casserole/Open, 12 Oz.	$5.00-7.00
114	Ice Jug, 2 Qt.	$25.00-28.00
115	Salt Shaker w/cork 3¾"	$6.00-8.00
116	Pepper Shaker w/cork, 3¾"	$6.00-8.00
118	Creamer or Jug, 8 Oz.	$7.00-12.00
119	Sugar Bowl w/cover, 12 Oz.	$7.00-12.00
121	Chip 'n Dip Leaf, 15" x 10½"	$25.00-35.00
122	Coffee Pot w/cover, 8 Cup	$35.00-45.00
123	Cookie Jar w/cover, 94 Oz.	$35.00-45.00
124	Indv. Bean Pot w/cover, 12 Oz.	$7.00-12.00
125	Jug, 2 Pt.	$24.00-29.00
126	Beer Stein, 16 Oz.	$8.00-10.00
127	Fr. Handle Indv. Casserole w/cover, 12 Oz.	$8.00-10.00
141	Indv. Oval Steak Plate, 11¾" x 9"	$12.00-15.00
142	Divided Vegetable Dish, 10¾" x 7¼"	$16.00-22.00
143	Oval Casserole, 2 Pt., 10" x 7¼" Open	$12.00-14.00
144	Oval Casserole w/cover, 3 Pt.	$18.00-22.00
145	Salad or Spaghetti Bowl, 10¼"	$23.00-27.00
148	Oval Casserole w/cover, 2 Qt.	$18.00-22.00
149	Tea Pot w/cover, 5 Cup	$25.00-30.00
151	Jam/Mustard Jar w/cover, 12 Oz.	$7.00-12.00
153	Soup Mug, 11 Oz.	$6.00-8.00
154	Tray for Snack Set	$4.00-5.00

Not Pictured:

No.	Description	Value
135	Bud Vase	$12.00-18.00
161	Butter Dish w/cover	$15.00-18.00
163	Ash Tray	$22.00-26.00
166	Pie Plate	$18.00-22.00

CRESTONE (Turquoise)

No.	Description	Value
300	Dinner Plate, 10¼"	$8.00-12.00
301	Dessert Plate, 7½"	$5.00-7.00
302	Coffee Cup (Mug) 9 Oz.	$5.00-6.00
303	Fruit Bowl, 6 "	$4.00-6.00
304	Bread 'n Butter Plate, 6½"	$4.00-5.00
305	Carafe, 2 Cup	$30.00-40.00
306	Open Baker	$14.00-18.00
307	Casserole w/lid, 32 Oz.	$20.00-25.00

CRESTONE *(Turquoise) (Continued)*

No.	Description	Value
308	Indv. Casserole w/cover, 9 Oz.	$16.00-20.00
310	Gravy Boat, 10 Oz.	$15.00-20.00
311	Gravy Boat Saucer	$10.00-12.00
313	Fr. Handled Indv. Casserole/Open, 9 Oz.	$8.00-12.00
314	Custard Cup, 6 Oz.	$8.00-10.00
315	Salt Shaker, 3¾"	$7.00-9.00
316	Pepper Shaker, 3¾"	$7.00-9.00
318	Creamer, 8 Oz.	$14.00-18.00
319	Sugar Bowl w/cover, 8 Oz.	$14.00-18.00
321	Chip 'n Dip Leaf, 14¼" x 10¼" x 2¼"	$35.00-40.00
322	Coffee Pot w/lid, 60 Oz.	$40.00-55.00
325	Pitcher, 38 Oz.	$40.00-50.00
326	Beer Stein, 14 Oz.	$12.00-18.00
327	Fr. Handled Indv. Casserole w/lid, 9 Oz.	$12.00-18.00
329	Coffee Cup, 7 Oz.	$4.00-6.00
330	Saucer, 5¾"	$3.00-5.00
331	Luncheon Plate, 9⅜"	$7.00-9.00
345	Vegetable or Salad Bowl, 9¾"	$18.00-28.00
349	Tea Pot w/cover, 5 Cup	$35.00-45.00
351	Jam/Mustard Jar w/cover	$14.00-18.00
361	Covered Butter Dish, ¼ lb.	$18.00-20.00
369	Onion Soup Bowl, 9 Oz.	$6.00-8.00
870C	Indv. Oval Steak Plate, 11¾" x 9"	$25.00-35.00
871C	Well 'n Tree Platter, 14" x 10"	$40.00-50.00

GINGERBREAD

No.	Description	Value
123	Gingerbread Man Cookie Jar/Gray	$175.00-220.00
198	Gingerbread Man Server 10" x l0"/Brown	$25.00-30.00
199	Gingerbread Man Coaster/Gray 5" x 5"	$25.00-30.00
223	Gingerbread Man Cookie Jar/Sand	$175.00-220.00
299	Gingerbread Man Coaster/Sand 5"x 5"	$25.00-30.00
323	Gingerbread Man Cookie Jar/Brown	$75.00-125.00
324	Gingerbread Man/Child's Cup	$70.00-80.00
325	Gingerbread Man/Child's Bowl	$70.00-80.00
399	Gingerbread Man Coaster/Brown 5" x 5"	$25.00-30.00
801G	Gingerbread Depot Cookie Jar	$125.00-150.00
802G	Gingerbread Train Set/Brown	SET
802G1	Gingerbread Train Engine	$400.00-500.00
802G2	Gingerbread Train Coal Car	$400.00-500.00
802G3	Gingerbread Train Passenger Car	$400.00-500.00
802G4	Gingerbread Train Caboose	$400.00-500.00
1198	Gingerbread Man Server l0" x l0"/Gray	$40.00-50.00
2198	Gingerbread Man Server 10" x l0"/Sand	$40.00-50.00

HEARTLAND
(Beige/Brown "Heart Stencil")

No.	Description	Value
400	Dinner Plate	$9.00-12.00
401	Salad Plate	$6.00-8.00
402	Coffee Cup	$6.00-7.00
403	Soup/Salad Bowl, 12 Oz.	$7.00-9.00
405	Saucer for Coffee Cup	$5.00-6.00
408	Oval Serving Bowl	$16.00-22.00
410	Bean Pot w/cover	$25.00-35.00
417	Souffle Dish	$25.00-29.00
418	Creamer	$10.00-15.00
419	Sugar Bowl	$12.00-16.00
422	Gravy Boat w/tray	$17.00-28.00
423	Cookie Jar	$38.00-48.00
428	Round Casserole w/cover	$30.00-40.00
436	Bowl, 6"	$12.00-18.00
438	Bowl, 8"	$15.00-22.00
440	Bowl, 10"	$22.00-26.00
441	Oval Platter	$22.00-25.00
442	Soup/Salad Bowl, 20 Oz.	$9.00-11.00
444	Quiche Dish	$18.00-28.00
449	Coffee Pot	$40.00-50.00
453	Salt/Pepper Set w/handles	$25.00-32.00
462	Unlabeled Condiment Server	$15.00-18.00
463	Cheese Server	$15.00-18.00
466	Round Baker/Cobbler Dish	$22.00-28.00
467	Rectangular Baker	$28.00-32.00
468	Square Baker	$14.00-18.00
470	Pitcher, 36 Oz.	$35.00-40.00
471	Stemmed Coffee Cup	$8.00-10.00
472	Pitcher, 66 Oz.	$42.00-57.00
473	109 Oz. Bowl/FOR BOWL & PITCHER	$35.00-45.00
476	Custard Cup	$6.00-8.00
490	Canister Set	$125.00-170.00
495	Handled Skillet	$22.00-28.00
4280	Oval Casserole w/Duck cover, 2 Pt.	$55.00-70.00
4850	Oval Cassernle w/Chicken cover, 2 Qt.	$55.00-70.00

HOUSE 'N GARDEN/MIRROR BROWN

No.	Description	Value
195	Corky Pig Bank	$25.00-30.00
196	Sitting Pig Bank	$25.00-30.00
197	Jumbo Corky Piggy Bank	$70.00-90.00
302	Mug, 10 Oz. (1980's)	$3.00-5.00
314	Round Casserole w/cover, (1980's)	$12.00-14.00
360	Canister Set, 4-Piece Stacking, (1980's)	$100.00-125.00

HOUSE 'N GARDEN/MIRROR BROWN *(Continued)*

No.	Description	Value
376	Custard Cup, 8 Oz.	$5.00-7.00
500	Dinner Plate, 10¼"	$3.00-5.00
501	Salad Plate, 6½"	$2.00-3.00
502	Coffee Cup, (Mug), 9 Oz.	$3.00-4.00
503	Fruit Bowl, 5¼"	$2.00-3.00
505	Carafe, 2 Cup	$18.00-22.00
507	Casserole w/lid, 32 Oz.	$12.00-15.00
508	Quiche Dish (1980's)	$22.00-26.00
508	Oval Salad Bowl w/Rooster imprint	$8.00-12.00
509	Water Jug, 5 Pt., 80 Oz.	$18.00-25.00
510	Bean Pot w/cover, 2 Qt.	$15.00-20.00
511	Gravy Boat	$12.00-14.00
512	Gravy Boat Saucer	$5.00-8.00
513	Fr. Handle Indv. Casserole/Open, (1980's)	$3.00-5.00
514	Ice Jug, 2 Qt.	$15.00-20.00
515	Salt Shaker w/cork, 3¾"	$3.00-4.00
517	Souffle Dish, (1980's)	$22.00-27.00
518	Creamer or Jug, 8 Oz. /10 Oz.	$3.00-4.00
519	Sugar Bowl w/cover, 12 Oz.	$3.00-5.00
521	Chip 'n Dip Leaf, 15" x 10½"	$15.00-20.00
522	Coffee Pot, 8 Cup	$18.00-25.00
523	Cookie Jar w/cover, 94 Oz.	$18.00-25.00
524	Indv. Bean Pot w/cover, 12 Oz.	$4.00-5.00
525	Jug, 2 Pt.	$12.00-14.00
526	Beer Stein, 16 Oz.	$4.00-6.00
527	Fr. Handle Indv. Casserole w/cover, (1980's)	$5.00-7.00
529	Coffee Cup, 6 Oz.	$3.00-5.00
530	Saucer, 5½"	$3.00-5.00
531	Luncheon Plate, 8½"	$7.00-9.00
533	Fruit Bowl, 6"	$3.00-5.00
534	Rectangular Baker, 7 Pt. Open	$35.00-40.00
535	Onion Soup Bowl w/cover, 12 Oz. (1980's)	$6.00-7.00
535	Rectangular Roaster w/cover, 7 Pt.	$60.00-90.00
536	Mixing Bowl, 6"	$4.00-6.00
537	Mixing Bowl, 7"	$7.00-9.00
538	Mixing Bowl, 8"	$10.00-12.00
540	Leaf Serve-All 12" x 7½"	$25.00-35.00
540	Gravy Boat & Saucer	$17.00-22.00
541	Indv. Oval Steak Plate, 11¾" x 9"	$7.00-9.00
542	Divided Vegetable Dish, 10¾" x 7¼"	$10.00-12.00
543	Oval Casserole 2 Pt., 10" x 7¼", Open	$5.00-8.00
544	Oval Casserole w/cover, 2 Pt.	$14.00-18.00
545	Salad or Spaghetti Bowl, 10¼"	$14.00-18.00
548	Oval Casserole w/cover, 2 Qt.	$16.00-20.00
549	Tea Pot w/cover, 5 Cup	$15.00-20.00
550	Jam/Mustard Jar w/cover, 13 Oz., (1980's)	$5.00-7.00
551	Jam/Mustard Jar w/cover, 12 Oz.	$5.00-7.00
553	Soup Mug, 11 Oz. & 14 Oz.	$4.00-5.00
554	Tray for Snack Set	$6.00-7.00
556	Canister, (Tea)	$45.00-60.00

No.	Description	Value
556	Cover/Chicken Top for Baker/Platter	$30.00-40.00
557	Canister, (Coffee)	$45.00-60.00
557	Oval Platter w/Rooster Imprint	$30.00-40.00
558	Baker/Open (Rooster Imprint), 3" Deep	$30.00-40.00
558	Canister, (Sugar)	$45.00-60.00
559	Canister, (Flour)	$45.00-60.00
559	Platter w/Chicken cover	$90.00-110.00
560	Baker Oval w/Chicken cover, 13" x 1l"	$90.00-110.00
561	Covered Butter Dish, ¼ lb.	$4.00-6.00
562	Fr. Handled Casserole/Open, 9 Oz., (New)	$3.00-4.00
563	Ash Tray w/Deer imprint, 8"	$15.00-20.00
565	Dutch Oven (2) Pieces, 3 Pt.	$20.00-25.00
566	Pie Plate, 9½" Dia.	$16.00-22.00
567	Rectangular Baker, (1980's)	$25.00-28.00
568	Square Baker, 3 Pt.	$8.00-10.00
569	Soup or Salad Bowl, 6½"	$4.00-6.00
571	Continental Mug, 10 Oz. & 12 Oz.	$7.00-9.00
572	Jumbo Stein, 32 Oz.	$25.00-35.00
573	Oval Bake 'n Serve Dish, 9½ Oz., (1980's)	$6.00-8.00
573	Corn Serving Dish, 9¼" x 3⅜"	$16.00-20.00
574	Oval Bake 'n Serve Dish, 16 Oz.	$6.00-8.00
576	Custard Cup, 6 Oz.	$6.00-8.00
577	Double Serving Dish/Scalloped	$35.00-40.00
579	Fr. Handled Casserole w/cover, 9 Oz. (New)	$4.00-6.00
579	Fr. Handled Casserole/lid & Warmer, 3 Pt.	$70.00-80.00
581	Indv. Oval Spaghetti, 10¾" x 8¼"	$9.00-11.00
582	Cheese Server	$12.00-18.00
583	Rectangular Salad Server, 11" x 6½"	$12.00-15.00
583	Chip 'n Dip (3 Sections)	$30.00-40.00
584	Sauce Bowl for Chips 'n Dip	$37.00-50.00
584	Oil Server	$12.00-18.00
585	Tray for Chip 'n Dip Set	$37.00-50.00
585	Vinegar Server	$12.00-18.00
586	Chip 'n Dip, 2 pieces, 12" x 11"	$75.00-100.00
587	Salt Shaker/Mushroom, 3¾"	$7.00-10.00
588	Pepper Shaker/Mushroom, 3¾"	$7.00-10.00
589	Bake 'n Serve, 6½" Round	$4.00-6.00
590	Indv. Leaf Dish, 7¼" x 4¼"	$5.00-7.00
591	Chip 'n Dip Leaf, 12¼" x 9"	$13.00-18.00
591	Deviled Egg Server w/Rooster Imprint	$15.00-22.00
592	Oval Hen on Nest	$50.00-65.00
592	Two-Tiered Tidbit	$22.00-28.00
593	Oval Well 'n Tree Steak Plate, 14" x 10"	$22.00-30.00
594	Spoon Rest/oval "Spoon Rest" imprint	$17.00-22.00
595	Handled Skillet	$10.00-12.00
596	Salt & Pepper Set, (Table Size) Set	$14.00-18.00
596	Fish Platter, 11"	$28.00-35.00
597	Coffee Cup, 7 Oz.	$3.00-5.00
598	Saucer, 5⅞"	$2.00-3.00
599	Luncheon Plate, 9⅜"	$7.00-9.00

HOUSE 'N GARDEN (Continued)

No.	Description	Value
600	Ramekin, 2½ Oz. (1980's)	$4.00-6.00
850H	Mixing Bowl, 5¼" (Provincial Mold)	$8.00-10.00
851H	Mixing Bowl, 6¾" (Provincial Mold)	$9.00-12.00
852H	Mixing Bowl, 8¼" (Provincial Mold)	$12.00-15.00
853H	Bake Dish/Casserole w/lid, (Provincial Mold)	$16.00-18.00
870H	Bud Vase, 9"	$14.00-18.00
871H	Rare Condiment Set	$75.00-100.00
872H	Rare Serving Set	$75.00-100.00
873H	Handled Server	$70.00-85.00
3505	Garlic Cellar, 13 Oz. (1980's)	$9.00-11.00
5280	Oval Casserole w/Duck cover, 2 Pt.	$45.00-60.00
5850	Oval Casserole w/Chicken cover, 2 Qt.	$45.00-60.00

IMPERIAL

NOTE: PRICES ALL COLORS

No.	Description	Values
A2	Square Footed Planter	$7.00-9.00
A6	Scroll Flower Dish	$7.00-8.00
A50	Rose Embossed Pitcher	$15.00-22.00
A54	Round Pedestal Planter	$6.00-8.00
A55	Footed Six-Sided Planter	$6.00-8.00
B6	Fancy Ruffled Bowl	$7.00-9.00
B34	Footed Garden Dish	$15.00-18.00
B36	Footed Basket	$25.00-30.00
F1	Bud Vase	$12.00-15.00
F5	Swirl Goblet Planter	$5.00-7.00
F10	Fluted Round Flower Bowl	$6.00-8.00
F17	Daisy Embossed Garden Dish	$6.00-8.00
F18	Fruit Embossed Garden Dish	$8.00-11.00
F34	Urn Shaped Planter	$6.00-8.00
F35	Cylindrical Vase	$8.00-12.00
F39	Fluted Oval Garden Dish	$5.00-6.00
F41	Rectangular Low Flower Bowl	$10.00-12.00
F42	Rectangular Fluted Garden Dish	$6.00-8.00
F47	Rectangular Garden Dish	$6.00-8.00
F48	Small Planter	$7.00-9.00
F49	Round Pedestal Planter	$5.00-7.00
F50	Round Pedestal Planter	$6.00-8.00
F51	Three Footed Pot	$7.00-9.00
F52	Footed Planter	$6.00-8.00
F53	Footed Round Bowl	$7.00-9.00
F54	Footed Round Bowl w/Lugs	$7.00-9.00
F55	Footed Six-Sided Embossed Planter	$7.00-9.00
F56	Footed Six-Sided Planter	$6.00-8.00
F57	Square Footed Planter	$6.00-8.00
F58	Vase With Flared Top	$12.00-15.00
F59	Round Paneled Bowl	$7.00-9.00

No.	Description	Value
F60	Round Paneled Bowl	$7.00-9.00
F61	Heart Shaped Garden Dish	$15.00-16.00
F62	Eight-Sided Footed Planter	$5.00-7.00
F63	Leaf Dish, 15" X 10½"	$18.00-22.00
F63	Oval Footed Bowl	$8.00-11.00
F64	Oval Vase	$14.00-18.00
F65	Oval Vase	$12.00-14.00
F65	Embossed Round Bowl	$15.00-18.00
F66	Oval Handled Basket	$25.00-40.00
F67	Wicker Embossed Handled Basket	$25.00-40.00
F68	Caricature Hippo Planter	$25.00-40.00
F69	Duck Planter	$25.00-40.00
F70	Caricature Frog	$25.00-40.00
F71	Swan Centerpiece	$25.00-40.00
F75	Garden Dish	$6.00-8.00
F76	Garden Dish	$6.00-8.00
F77	Fancy Oval Garden Dish	$7.00-8.00
F78	Rectangular Leaf Design Garden Dish	$7.00-9.00
F83	Pressed Pedestal Planter	$6.00-7.00
F88	Sculptured Pedestal Planter	$7.00-9.00
F90	Single Bud Vase	$7.00-9.00
F91	Bowl & Pitcher/Centennial Eagle Design	$12.00-18.00
F401	Low Round Flower Bowl	$6.00-8.00
F404	Footed Garden Dish	$5.00-6.00
F405	Footed Flower Dish	$5.00-6.00
F410	Pedestaled Flower Bowl	$9.00-12.00
F411	Square Footed Planter	$9.00-12.00
F412	Urn Planter	$9.00-12.00
F416	Bell Vase	$12.00-15.00
F422	Oriental Planter	$7.00-9.00
F425	Octagonal Compote	$8.00-11.00
F430	Footed Round Flower Bowl	$8.00-10.00
F432	Chalice Vase	$12.00-15.00
F433	Pedestaled Ivy Vase	$15.00-18.00
F434	Urn Vase	$9.00-12.00
F435	Bud Vase	$10.00-15.00
F436	Float Bowl Console	$14.00-18.00
F439	Usubata Vase	$15.00-18.00
F445	Candle Holders (Pair)	$20.00-30.00
F447	Paneled Garden Dish	$5.00-6.00
F467	Fluted Garden Dish	$6.00-8.00
F469	Paneled Garden Dish	$6.00-8.00
F478	Round Centerpiece Ped. Flower Bowl	$6.00-8.00
I21	Oval Fluted Garden Dish	$5.00-6.00
815I	Swan Ash Tray	$7.00-10.00
890I	Pedestal Flower Bowl	$7.00-9.00
891I	Rectangular Footed Flower Dish	$7.00-9.00
892I	Long Stem Vase	$14.00-19.00
893I	Candy Dish/Centerpiece	$9.00-12.00
894I	Circle H "Basketweave" Planter	$18.00-24.00
895I	Bunny Candy Dish	$250.00-300.00

MIRROR ALMOND

No.	Description	Value
800	Dinner Plate, 10¼"	$9.00-12.00
801	Salad Plate, 6½"	$6.00-7.00
802	Mug, 9 Oz.	$5.00-6.00
803	Fruit Bowl, 5¼"	$5.00-6.00
804	Luncheon Plate, 8½"	$7.00-9.00
805	Cup, 6 oz.	$5.00-6.00
806	Ramekin, 2½ Oz .	$7.00-8.00
807	Gingerbread Serving Tray, (Rare)	$38.00-45.00
808	Vinegar Cruet, 5¾"	$22.00-30.00
818	Creamer, 10 Oz.	$14.00-18.00
819	Sugar Bowl w/lid	$14.00-18.00
826	Beer Stein, 16 Oz.	$15.00-18.00
827	Indiv. French Handled Casserole w/lid	$12.00-16.00
836	Mixing Bowl, 6"	$10.00-12.00
837	Mixing Bowl, 7"	$14.00-16.00
838	Mixing Bowl w/lid, 8"	$16.00-20.00
841	Oval Steak Plate, 11¾" x 9"	$15.00-18.00
842	Divided Vegetable, 10¾" x 7¾"	$14.00-18.00
853	Soup Mug, 11 Oz.	$10.00-14.00
854	Tray or Snack Set, 9½" x 5¾"	$10.00-14.00
867	Handled Vegetable Server	$14.00-16.00
869	Soup or Salad Bowl, 6½"	$5.00-6.00
873	Small Oval Serving Dish, 8¾" x 4"	$7.00-12.00
887	Mushroom Salt Shaker, 3¾"	$10.00-13.00
888	Mushroom Pepper Shaker, 3¾"	$10.00-13.00

MISCELLANEOUS

No.	Description	Value
890M	Handled Casserole	$30.00-40.00
891M	Covered Bowl	$25.00-35.00
897M	Coffee Cup	$9.00-11.00
898M	Coffee Pot	$35.00-50.00
899M	Casserole	$30.00-40.00
1001M	Ash Tray Eight-Sided (Employee Special)	$35.00-40.00
1002M	Mug, 9 Oz. (Purdue University Imprint)	$9.00-12.00
1003M	Beer Stein, 16 Oz. (Tremont Nail Co.)	$10.00-15.00
1004M	Bean Pot, 2 Qt. (Boston Baked Beans Imp.)	$22.00-28.00
1005M	Imprinted, 16 Oz. Mugs	$15.00-20.00
1006M	Imprinted Continental Mugs	$15.00-20.00
1007M	Test Cups	$3.00-6.00
1008M	Ash Tray, Experimental	$45.00-60.00
1009M	Heart-Shaped Ash Tray	$25.00-30.00
1010M	Souffle Dish (Country Squire/Agate)	$32.00-38.00
1011M	Experimental Pitcher (Mirror Brown)	$250.00-300.00
1012M	Hull Plaque (Ohio Pottery Museum)	$30.00-40.00
1013M	Unknown Turtle Planter	$60.00-80.00
1014M	Unknown Fish Planter	$20.00-25.00
1015M	Chickadee Planter (F473) Mirror Brown	$20.00-25.00
1016M	Divided Server, 11" 1980's	$25.00-30.00
1017M	Cook 'n Serve Handled Skillet	$45.00-60.00
1018M	Experimental (F433 Adaption) Vase	$75.00-90.00

PROVINCIAL
(Two-Tone Brown & White)

No.	Description	Value
700	Dinner Plate, 10¼"	$12.00-15.00
701	Salad Plate, 6½"	$8.00-11.00
702	Coffee Cup, (Mug), 9 Oz.	$7.00-9.00
702P	Saucer	$5.00-7.00
703	Fruit Bowl, 5¼"	$7.00-10.00
705	Mixing Bowl, 5¼"	$10.00-12.00
706	Mixing Bowl, 6¾"	$15.00-20.00
707	Mixing Bowl, 8¼"	$18.00-22.00
709	Water Jug, 5 Pt., 80 Oz.	$35.00-45.00
710	Bean Pot w/cover, 2 Qt.	$35.00-45.00
711	Bake Dish, 3 Pt.	$18.00-22.00
712	Bake Dish w/cover, 3 Pt./Warmer	$22.00-27.00
713	Fr. Handle Indv. Casserole/Open, 12 Oz.	$10.00-12.00
714	Ice Jug, 2 Qt.	$25.00-35.00
715	Salt Shaker w/cork, 3¾"	$10.00-12.00
716	Pepper Shaker w/cork, 3¾"	$10.00-12.00
718	Creamer or Jug, 8 Oz.	$12.00-16.00
719	Sugar Bowl w/cover, 12 Oz.	$12.00-18.00
721	Chip n Dip Leaf, 15" x 10½"	$30.00-35.00
722	Coffee Pot w/cover, 8 Cup	$40.00-50.00
723	Cookie Jar w/cover, 94 Oz.	$40.00-55.00
724	Indv. Bean Pot w/cover, 12 Oz.	$12.00-18.00
725	Jug, 2 Pt.	$22.00-28.00
726	Beer Stein, 16 Oz.	$15.00-22.00
727	Fr. Handle Indv. Casserole w/cover, 12 Oz.	$14.00-18.00

RAINBOW
(Tangerine/Green, Agate/Butterscotch & Brown)

NOTE: SEE HOUSE 'N GARDEN/MIRROR BROWN FOR BROWN RAINBOW

No.	Description	Value
232RA	Coffee Cup, 6 Oz. (Colors)	$4.00-6.00
233RA	Saucer, 5½" (Colors)	$3.00-4.00
234RA	Luncheon Plate, 8½" (Colors)	$7.00-9.00
235RA	Salad Plate, (Butterscotch)	$4.00-5.00
260RA	Coffee Cup, (Mug), 9 Oz. (Colors)	$5.00-6.00
261RA	Dinner Plate, 10½" (Colors)	$7.00-9.00
262RA	Soup & Salad Bowl, 6½" (Colors)	$5.00-7.00
536	Mixing Bowl, 6" (Colors)	$7.00-10.00
537	Mixing Bowl, 7" (Colors)	$8.00-12.00
538	Mixing Bowl, 8" (Colors)	$12.00-16.00
540	Leaf Serve-All, 12" x 7½" (Colors)	$35.00-45.00
590	Indv. Leaf Dish, 7¼" x 4¼" (Colors)	$7.00-8.00
591	Chip 'n Dip Leaf, 12¼" x 9" (Colors)	$25.00-35.00
592	Two Tier Tidbit (All Colors)	$25.00-32.00
861RA	Soup Mug, 11 Oz. (Butterscotch)	$6.00-8.00
862RA	Tray for Snack Set (Butterscotch)	$4.00-5.00

RIDGE *(Flint Ridge/gray)*

No.	Description	Value
100	Dinner Plate, 10¼"	$6.00-8.00
101	Salad Plate, 7¼"	$4.00-5.00
102	Mug, 10 Oz.	$3.00-5.00
103	Bowl, 5½" x 2½", 18 Oz.	$4.00-6.00
104	Cup, 8 Oz.	$4.00-5.00
105	Saucer, 6"	$3.00-5.00
107	Tray, 7" x 9½"	$12.00-16.00
108	Vegetable Server, 7½" x 2½", 32 Oz.	$7.00-9.00
109	Sugar Bowl w/cover, 8 Oz.	$8.00-10.00
110	Creamer, 8 Oz.	$8.00-10.00
111	Salt Shaker, 2½" x 3"	$7.00-9.00
113	Pepper Shaker, 2½" x 3"	$7.00-9.00
115	Steak Plate, 9½" x 12"	$8.00-11.00

RIDGE *(Tawny Ridge/Sand)*

No.	Description	Value
200	Dinner Plate, 10¼ "	$6.00-8.00
201	Salad Plate, 7¼ "	$4.00-5.00
202	Mug, 10 Oz.	$3.00-5.00
203	Bowl, 5½" x 2½", 18 Oz.	$4.00-6.00
204	Cup, 8 Oz.	$4.00-5.00
205	Saucer, 6"	$3.00-5.00
207	Tray, 7" x 9½"	$12.00-16.00
208	Vegetable Server, 7½" x 2½", 32 Oz.	$8.00-10.00
209	Sugar Bowl w/cover, 8 Oz.	$8.00-10.00
210	Creamer, 8 Oz.	$7.00-9.00
211	Salt Shaker, 2½" x 3"	$7.00-9.00
213	Pepper Shaker, 2½" x 3"	$7.00-9.00
215	Steak Plate, 9½" x 12"	$8.00-11.00

RIDGE *(Walnut Ridge/Brown)*

No.	Description	Value
300	Dinner Plate, 10¼"	$6.00-8.00
301	Salad Plate, 7¼"	$4.00-5.00
302	Mug, 10 Oz.	$3.00-5.00
303	Bowl, 5½" x 2½", 18 Oz.	$4.00-6.00
304	Cup, 8 Oz.	$4.00-5.00
305	Saucer, 6"	$3.00-5.00
307	Tray, 7" x 9½"	$12.00-16.00
308	Vegetable Server, 7½" x 2½", 32 Oz.	$7.00-9.00
309	Sugar Bowl w/cover, 8 Oz.	$8.00-10.00
310	Creamer, 8 Oz.	$8.00-10.00
311	Salt Shaker, 2½" x 3"	$7.00-9.00
313	Pepper Shaker, 2½" x 3"	$7.00-9.00
315	Steak Plate, 9½" x 12"	$8.00-11.00

RING *(Brown)*

No.	Description	Value
5400	Dinner Plate	$9.00-12.00
5401	Salad Plate	$5.00-7.00
5402	Coffee Cup	$6.00-7.00
5403	Soup/Salad Bowl, 12 Oz.	$7.00-9.00
5405	Saucer for Coffee Cup	$5.00-6.00
5408	Oval Serving Bowl	$14.00-16.00
5410	Bean Pot w/cover	$25.00-35.00
5418	Creamer	$10.00-12.00
5419	Sugar Bowl	$10.00-12.00
5422	Gravy Boat w/tray	$17.00-25.00
5423	Cookie Jar	$28.00-35.00
5428	Round Casserole w/cover	$28.00-35.00
5436	Mixing Bowl, 6"	$10.00-12.00
5438	Mixing Bowl, 8"	$12.00-15.00
5440	Mixing Bowl, 10"	$18.00-22.00
5441	Oval Platter	$15.00-18.00
5442	Soup/Salad Bowl, 20 Oz.	$9.00-11.00
5449	Coffee Pot	$40.00-50.00
5453	Salt & Pepper Set w/handles	$22.00-28.00
5462	Cheese Server	$15.00-18.00
5466	Round Baker/Cobbler Dish	$18.00-21.00
5470	Pitcher, 36 Oz.	$30.00-35.00
5471	Stemmed Coffee Cup	$7.00-9.00
5472	Pitcher, 66 Oz.	$35.00-42.00
5473	109 Oz., Bowl/FOR BOWL & PITCHER	$35.00-45.00
5476	Custard Cup	$6.00-8.00
5490	Canister Set	$110.00-145.00

TANGERINE

No.	Description	Value
900	Dinner Plate, 10¼"	$7.00-9.00
901	Salad Plate 6½"	$4.00-5.00
902	Coffee Cup, Mug, 9 Oz.	$5.00-6.00
903	Fruit Bowl, 5¼"	$3.00-5.00
909	Water Jug, 5 Pt., 80 Oz.	$28.00-32.00
910	Bean Pot w/cover, 2 Qt.	$22.00-28.00
913	Fr. Handle Indv. Casserole/Open, 12 Oz.	$5.00-7.00
914	Ice Jug, 2 Qt.	$25.00-28.00
915	Salt Shaker w/cork, 3¾"	$6.00-8.00
916	Pepper Shaker w/cork, 3¾"	$6.00-8.00
918	Creamer or Jug, 8 Oz.	$7.00-12.00
919	Sugar Bowl w/cover, 12 Oz.	$7.00-12.00
921	Chip 'n Dip Leaf, 15" x 10½"	$25.00-35.00
922	Coffee Pot w/cover, 8 Cup	$35.00-45.00
923	Cookie Jar w/cover, 94 Oz.	$35.00-45.00
924	Indv. Bean Pot w/cover, 12 Oz.	$7.00-12.00
925	Jug, 2 Pt.	$24.00-29.00

TANGERINE *(Continued)*

No.	Description	Value
926	Beer Stein, 16 Oz.	$8.00-10.00
927	Fr. Handle Indv. Casserole w/cover, 12 Oz.	$8.00-10.00
935	Bud Vase (Imperial), 9"	$12.00-18.00
941	Indv. Oval Steak Plate, 11¾" x 9"	$12.00-15.00
942	Divided Vegetable Dish, 10¾" x 7¼"	$16.00-22.00
944	Oval Casserole w/cover, 2 Pt.	$18.00-22.00
945	Salad or Spaghetti Bowl, 10¼"	$23.00-27.00
948	Oval Casserole w/cover, 2 Qt.	$18.00-22.00
949	Tea Pot w/cover, 5 Cup	$25.00-30.00
951	Jam/Mustard Jar w/cover, 12 Oz.	$7.00-12.00
953	Soup Mug, 11 Oz.	$6.00-8.00
954	Tray for Snack Set	$4.00-5.00
961	Covered Butter Dish, ¼ lb.	$15.00-18.00
963	Ash Tray w/Deer imprint, 8"	$22.00-26.00
965	Dutch Oven, 2 Pieces, 3 Pt.	$25.00-30.00
966	Pie Plate, 9¼" Dia.	$18.00-22.00
969	Soup or Salad Bowl, 6½"	$5.00-7.00
979	Fr. Handled Casserole/lid & Warmer, 3 Pt.	$80.00-100.00

BIBLIOGRAPHY

Bauer, Louise. Personal correspondence, interviews 1992.

Duke, Harvey. Personal correspondence, interviews. 1991-1992.

Dunn, Opal. Personal correspondence, interviews. 1991-1992.

Dusenberry, Gene. Personal interview, brochures. 1991.

Felkner, Sharon. *"Lovely Hull Pottery."*

Frash, Royce & Stella. Personal interviews. 1991-1992.

Garrett, Grey. Personal interviews. 1991-1992.

Hull, Joan Gray. *"Hull the Heavenly Pottery."*

Hull, Joan Gray. Private correspondence, interviews. 1991-1992.

Roberts, Brenda. Telephone correspondence. 1991.

Roberts, Brenda. *"Ultimate Encyclopedia of Hull Pottery."*

Roberts, Brenda. *"The Collectors Encyclopedia of Hull Pottery."*

Taylor, Larry. Personal interviews, brochures. 1991-1992.

Schroeder's ANTIQUES Price Guide

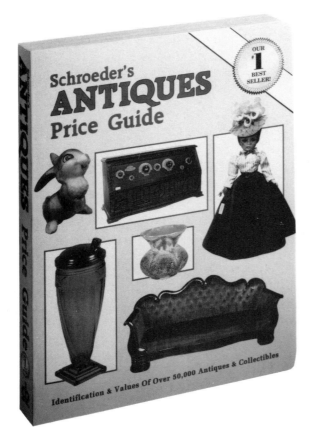

Schroeder's Antiques Price Guide is the #1 best-selling antiques & collectibles value guide on the market today, and here's why . . . More than 300 authors, well-known dealers, and top-notch collectors work together with our editors to bring you accurate information regarding pricing and identification. More than 45,000 items in almost 500 categories are listed along with hundreds of sharp original photos that illustrate not only the rare and unusual, but the common, popular collectibles as well. Each large close-up shot shows important details clearly. Every subject is represented with histories and background information, a feature not found in any of our competitors' publications. Our editors keep abreast of newly-developing trends, often adding several new categories a year as the need arises. If it merits the interest of today's collector, you'll find it in *Schroeder's*. And you can feel confident that the information we publish is up to date and accurate. Our advisors thoroughly check each category to spot inconsistencies, listings that may not be entirely reflective of market dealings, and lines too vague to be of merit. Only the best of the lot remains for publication. Without doubt, you'll find *Schroeder's Antiques Price Guide* the only one to buy for reliable information and values.

8½ x 11", 608 Pages   **$12.95**

COLLECTOR BOOKS
A Division of Schroeder Publishing Co., Inc.